This book's godly principles change lives

Readers have written to the author, saying:

—"I can't tell you how powerful my prayers have become since I've incorporated your understanding of binding and loosing. I plan to reread ***Shattering Your Strongholds*** several times to get all of the rich information out of it."

—"Your words about loosing the layers of self-protection and denial we've erected in trying to control our own pain and burying our own unmet needs was just the wisdom I needed to hear. Clearly, that's pro-typical of what I've done throughout my life, and that needs to be dealt with. Thank you."

—"The first third of your book is instructional, the second third peeled me like an onion, and the last third is bringing me and my loved ones to victory. My struggle in my emotions has been like a 20-year Vietnam. War was never declared, but there was always a battle going on. My life, in my mind's eye, was a barren, smoking battlefield, with ever fresh signs of recent bomb strikes still smoking. In the midst of all of this, I allowed the kingdom of self to begin to take territory in my spirit. [...] I have bought all the copies I can afford and given them out, encouraging everyone else to get a copy of ***Shattering Your Strongholds.*** This information has given me the greatest victory in my prayer life that I have ever experienced in 25 years of being a Christian!"

—"When you autographed my book, I told you that I had been trying to quit smoking for a long time with no success. You said smoking was just a symptom, that I had some strongholds I needed to deal with. Boy, were you right! Praise God for what He taught you in order to help others. No more cigarettes and no desire."

—"I've been avidly praying the ***Shattering Your Strongholds*** principles for about three years now, and right from the beginning I saw tangible and spectacular results—not only in my life, but in those to whom I've passed the teaching on to. I was hung up in my inner man in many ways. As I learned from ***Shattering Your Strongholds*** that God had given me weapons to destroy those wrong beliefs and thought patterns, freedom and clarity of thought arose rapidly. There's such power and stability to binding yourself to the steady and fixed things of God."

By the same author:

Breaking the Power

. . . the sequel to *Shattering Your Strongholds,* filled with greater spiritual insight into the power of the unsurrendered soul, erronious spiritual warfare and how to effectively use the keys of the kingdom—binding and loosing

Shattering Your Strongholds Workbook

. . . an 8 1/2 X 11 inch companion book with a question and answer format for individual or group study

For further information on speaking engagements, seminars, current U.S. itinerary, teaching tapes, workbooks, television programs and free teaching newsletters published quarterly, please contact:

Liberty Savard Ministries, Inc.
(a non-profit organization)
P.O. Box 41260
Sacramento, CA 95841-0260

E-mail: liberty@libertysavard.com
Web site: http://www.libertysavard.com

Office phone: 916-721-7770
Fax: 916-721-8889

SHATTERING YOUR STRONGHOLDS

Freedom From Your Struggles

Liberty Savard

Bridge-Logos *Publishers*

Gainesville, Florida 32614 USA

Shattering Your Strongholds by Liberty Savard

Library of Congress Catalog Card Number: 92-74981

International Standard Book Number: 0-88270-713-2

Reprinted 2004

Printed in the USA by:

Bridge-Logos

Gainesville, FL 32614

bridgelogos.com

To my two faithful friends who prayed with and encouraged me, often on a daily basis, walking the final miles with me to bring this book to completion:

Marian Johnson and Jan Hammond

Contents

Preface

Every believer in Christ Jesus has obtained an equal privilege of receiving whatsoever the Bible promises. Our God is no respecter of persons and the basis of His giving is not determined by a sliding scale of who is, who is not or when one finally becomes worthy of receiving what He has promised. To God the Father, a believer is worthy to receive simply because he or she is in His Son, Jesus Christ.

If you have accepted Jesus Christ as your Savior and Lord, you have the privilege of receiving spiritual wisdom, power, authority, understanding, answers and peace right now. Your heavenly Father has no desire to withhold any good thing from you. If you do not have these attributes, gifts and fruit in your life, it is not God who has opposed your receiving them. Nor can you blame the devil, your parents, your spouse, your relatives, your boss or your friends. It is you who has opposed yourself.

We've all wondered why some believers seem to have so much spiritually and others seem to have so little. The church world has been explaining this inequity for years with the teaching that God's gifts are dispensed when one meets certain "conditions" or levels of service, prayer, study, etc. But God has not made the manifestation of His promises contingent on any of man's conditions.

We can be most grateful that the Lord does not realign His faithfulness to conform to our concepts of His probable behavior. His faithfulness to His promises exists because He exists. Our dedication to service, prayer and study does not increase His faithfulness to His Word. True dedication simply comes from a heart that has been able to receive—a heart that is so full of thanksgiving, understanding, love and worship, it cannot do anything less.

What is the difference between those who seem to receive so much from the Lord and those who do not? The main difference is in how much room the recipients have made within themselves to receive. Those who receive much have stripped off, torn down and moved out the trappings of their old natures, thereby enlarging their capacity to receive. Having done this, they have ceased to oppose themselves and God's work in their lives. Every believer shares an equal privilege, right and ability to strip off, tear down and move out the old to enlarge his or her capacity to receive.

The Lord stands at the door knocking, wanting to bring in the abundance He has been waiting to give you. May the following words be the keys to unlock your understanding that you will make room to receive.

Acknowledgments

I wish to first thank my mother and father, Betty and Bill Savercool, who watched and wondered and waited during the years I struggled to birth this book. Thanks for all your help, Mom and Dad.

I also want to acknowledge and express my gratefulness to "Sarah" and her mother, who were willing to share their story so that others might be helped.

A very special thank you to all who asked the hard questions which brought forth new depth in the understanding.

And last, but not least, I want to thank my friend, Joan, who believed in the message.

CHAPTER 1

Keys to the Kingdom

The Truth Will Set You Free

Have you ever seen a time when so many were so wary of the truth of today's media headlines? Are we getting facts or fiction? It really is very hard to tell anymore. Does anyone mean what they are promising? Who knows?

"Nothing is what it seems. What is the truth?" cries the world.

Christians know the truth. Jesus died so that we could be forgiven and go to heaven. That is rock-solid, life-giving truth. Many Christians will make it all the way through life and home to God on that truth alone. They may not impact other lives and change the world, but that truth is enough to get them out of spending eternity in hell. Providing, of course, that they are not hit with any brutal or harsh circumstances that have to be lived out and walked through while they are still here on earth.

Life has a way of doing that sometimes. When it does, the strongest of Christians need every bit of truth they can get. This is a book about seeking for truth, whole truth—the deeper truth that comes with a price, but brings great reward.

Too many Christians quit seeking when surface truth brings them temporary blessings or relief. This one-dimension understanding costs little and requires little growth. Learning whole truth can bring growing pains, but God gives growth in stages we can handle. He has said to seek and we would find, so our command is to keep seeking. Those who do will feel growing pains when their capacity to receive becomes too small.

Think back to when you were little and remember the new dress shoes your mother bought for you. They were shiny and new and probably a little too big, but you could walk in them. After a certain length of time, they began to pinch and you had to step into a larger size. There was nothing wrong with the shoes, but your feet had grown. You needed more room.

That is the way it is with our understanding of God's multi-faceted, ever-expanding truths. If we are always seeking truth, we grow spiritually and when this happens, our size "1" understanding becomes too tight. So God says, *"You're ready to walk in this size '2' understanding now and I also want you to increase your solid foods. Try chewing on this piece of filet mignon for a while."*

Baby Christians are initially fed on the sincere milk of the Word of God because they cannot chew anything. Babies know only how to swallow. First Peter 2:2 (KJV) tells the new believer, "As newborn babes, desire the sincere milk of the word, that ye may grow thereby." Try feeding a baby Christian the stronger truths of the crucified flesh, dying to self and submission and he'll choke. You'll have to thump him on the back and spiritually burp him!

You feed a baby Christian on love, joy, answered prayer, guardian angels, blessings, heaven, etc. He can swallow that kind of spiritual milk—for a season. But, if he tries to stay on milk indefinitely, he will never be more than a baby.

The spiritually mature Christian cannot survive on a diet of milk. This believer needs and is trained to chew, swallow and digest meat without choking. "Anyone who lives on milk, being still an infant, is not acquainted with the teaching about righteousness. But solid food is for the mature, who by constant use have trained themselves to distinguish good from evil" (Heb. 5:13-14 NIV).

One fact about milk and meat reveals an interesting spiritual principle. Spoiled milk might make you sick, but it will rarely kill you. The milk of the Word can be accidentally spoiled if a baby Christian handles it improperly and still not bring spiritual death. We have all known new believers who made seriously wrong decisions based upon misinterpretations of the Word and still moved on in their relationship with God. They might get a spiritual tummy ache, but a dose of God's liquid grace gets them back on their feet.

Spoiled meat, on the other hand, can kill you. A believer who handles spiritual meat in such a way as to spoil its true meaning, misrepresenting God's standards of holiness and twisting His truth, can bring death. The meat of the Word must be handled with clean hands, pure hearts and a renewed mind.

Old Mind Sets

Every believer comes to Christ with certain old mind sets of misinformation. If these mind sets are deeply entrenched and resistant to renewal, a believer can come dangerously close to mishandling God's Word. Inside every one of us is a picture of God formed by what we have read, what we have been taught, our personal experiences and our past memories and feelings. We can actually have two pictures of God—what we learn we should believe about Him and what we actually do believe.

What you learn about God has to filter down through the existing beliefs in your mind. This fact is not always understood by Christians, laypeople and leadership alike. Many in leadership assume scripturally correct teaching will automatically clear up any wrong ideas someone might have about God. Theoretically, scripturally correct teaching on trust, love and faith should enable anyone to trust and love God with complete faith. And it usually will—eventually.

The problem is, even scripturally correct truth cannot always penetrate a soul that is filled with strongholds. God can sovereignly impart revelation knowledge any time He wants to, but I believe His work of renewal occurs within the framework of our minds, wills, emotions, memories, experiences and beliefs. He does not change, bypass or override, He just keeps offering

His love and truth until we finally become willing to exchange our old beliefs and ideas for them.

An unrenewed mind, rigid in mind sets formed from wrong sources, can distort the most beautiful spiritual truth. The Christian's mind is not automatically renewed at the point of new birth. This is why there must be a continuing process of washing in the Word.

Self-Erected Strongholds

Most minds come into the state of salvation stubbornly filled with old attitudes, wrong patterns of thinking and some pretty strange ideas. Many of these old ideas and attitudes will be protected by self-erected strongholds.

The key to receiving renewal as fast as possible is to tear down the strongholds around these wrong mind sets. Unfortunately, some Christians never accomplish this; instead, they may spend their entire lives trying to intermingle their concepts of God with His truth.

Even the Old Testament prophets were subject to hearing certain things through old mind sets. God did not automatically create perfect, undistorted vessels to become His prophets; He worked through people just like you and me. Consider Elijah, the great prophet of fire, who fled into the desert to hide from Jezebel. He had just faced down hundreds of prophets of Baal on Mount Carmel and called down heavenly fire from above, but something in Elijah caused him to fall apart before Jezebel's threat. He had an old mind set that defeated him when the right circumstance played out.

Many Christians have formed their concept of God from old ideas rather than the truth. This is why some believers never seem to get past believing that God accepts them when they measure up and angrily turns away when they fail. There are untold numbers who have never truly accepted God as a nurturing and loving parent always ready to encourage their development. Rather, they picture Him as saying, *"Nope, that's still not good enough."* This does not come from God. It comes from an old mind set that keeps them from receiving the truth.

No matter how discouraged you might be right now, you can be free of the old mind sets and distortions in your "understanding." Jesus gave the keys to tear down and strip away these flawed concepts, wrong ideas, doubts and distortions. He knew that once we had forgiveness and the gift of eternal life, we still had to live out our days on this earth. Jesus Christ was well aware that our days would be spent dealing with an enemy who is determined to destroy our relationship with God. Jesus knew we needed the power of truth to overcome this enemy.

Jesus experienced pain, want, hunger, fatigue, sorrow and loss. He knew the sting of rejection, animosity and sarcasm. He knows exactly what life feels like as a baby, a child, a teenager and an adult. We are told in Galatians that in Christ Jesus there is no distinction between male and female (Gal. 3:28). In other words, He knows exactly how both men and women feel. And because He did not suddenly come into this world as a full-grown Savior, the child and the teenager can know that Christ understands their feelings, too.

I remember seeing a Ziggy cartoon where Ziggy stood looking in frustration towards heaven, saying, "It's not easy being mortal, you know!" Jesus knows that. He knows what He needed as a mortal. He has always known that we would need keys of kingdom power to overcome our former lives and the devil to face our future. We have a definite reason for having a future, you know. We are not spiritual experiments like bugs in a test tube. We are not here to be scored on how well we do. We are here to show God's love to the world. He has given His Son's power and authority to us so that we can.

Too many in the Church today see themselves in terms of their pasts, their upbringing, their shattered marriages, their lost jobs, their lack of money, etc. They don't see themselves in terms of their potential in Christ. They need brothers and sisters who will say, "You need to see yourself like God sees you. I know a way to pray with you so you can see yourself that way."

The world needs people who will say, "You can turn your discouragement and hurt into an open doorway leading into Jesus Christ's arms and be healed. Or you can let your pain drive you into a blind corner. I know a way we can pray to help you become whole and strong."

The body of Christ needs people who will say, "You cannot rate God's love or His promises by your unanswered prayer. The problem's not in Him, but we often oppose ourselves. Let me help you pray."

I'm not saying you should withhold love and compassion; I'm suggesting you work on the "whatsoevers" in their lives to bring them into their status as new creatures in Christ. Love them and work with them if they will let you. Love them and work without their cooperation if they won't. You can have an impact on peoples' lives even without their permission. You can pray very effectively for God's will and purposes and the truth, "behind their backs."

The New Creature Process

The Bible clearly states, in the tenth chapter of Romans, that when we have confessed with our mouths that Jesus is Lord and believe in our hearts that God raised Him from the dead, we are saved. It also states that when we are saved, we are new creatures. A new creature with old things passed away has the right to be free from the past.

This is truth and I hope you believe it for exactly what it says. But this truth involves a process and because the enemy of your soul hates truth, he's going to do his best to gum up that process. Once the beautiful excitement of forgiveness, salvation and your awareness of Jesus settles down into the daily Christian walk, Satan quietly begins to chip away at your new identity.

As believers, we are new creatures in old, unresurrected bodies. We are still in the flesh with a new nature indwelt by the Spirit of God. What a dichotomy! As the new spiritual nature begins to grow in you, the trouble begins. Your old nature is sharply aware that something has suddenly appeared on the scene that could be totally disastrous to the free rein it has held in your life and it responds vehemently. It is no wonder that a Christian can feel totally undone at times!

But Jesus has made provision for us to walk into renewal and restoration right here on earth while we are still in our mortal bodies. Titus 3:5 (NIV) says, "He saved us, not because of righteous things we had done, but because of his mercy. He saved us through the washing of rebirth and renewal by the Holy Spirit." Many have experienced the rebirth, but still hold on tight to their old ways just in case the renewal is delayed.

We hold all the covenant rights and we can override Satan and loose his bondages whenever we choose. This is God's will. But your will has to make a choice to call your life on earth into alignment with God's will in heaven. God will not force you to do so, but He will help you. "It is God Who is all the while effectually at work in you—energizing and creating in you the power and desire—both to will and to work for His good pleasure and satisfaction and delight" (Phil. 2:13 TAB). This is God's plan.

A Hope and a Future

Satan's plan is to drag you down, weighting you with lies and distortions unto the breaking of your will. He strives to convince you that you have no right to sonship with Jesus Christ. He strives to drag you under and prevent you from believing the God who says, "...I know the plans I have for you...plans to prosper you and not to harm you, plans to give you hope and a future" (Jer. 29:11 NIV).

This Scripture holds the promise of being prospered, having hope and a future filled with God's good plans. Could anyone resist that? Yes, it is resisted every day by those who are afraid to believe (believers and the non-believers alike), those who base their understanding of God upon the negative experiences of their lives.

It is time to get down to the basics of changing and impacting lives for God—your life and other lives—believers' lives and unbelievers' lives. The following words represent what the Lord has revealed to me as the unpracticed principles of one of His truths. At first it may appear to be in conflict with what you have been taught, but there is no reason or intent to conflict with other prayer and spiritual warfare concepts. Rather, this understanding is "the rest of the truth," as Paul Harvey would say. Search the Scriptures to see whether or not the Word of God agrees.

This is an understanding that has come slowly and carefully over six years. God's timing has kept me from running too fast with it and from being tempted to offer it in bits and pieces like buckshot. I believe God has said it is time. What I share will set that new creature in you free. It will bring understanding. It will enhance the effectiveness of your prayers and spiritual warfare. You will be able to tear down the strongholds you have built.

The Keys of the Kingdom

In 1985, God began to shake my understanding of Jesus' words in Matthew 16:19 (KJV): "And I will give unto thee the keys of the kingdom of heaven: and whatsoever thou shalt bind on earth shall be bound in heaven: and whatsoever thou shalt loose on earth shall be loosed in heaven."

Jesus spoke these words in Matthew 16:19 and 18:18, revealing a spiritual principle to those who believed in Him. "Heaven" here is the same Greek word as used in the other Gospels to denote the abode of God. It is the same word used in the references by Jesus to the "kingdom of heaven" and "our Father which is in heaven." Whatsoever we bind on earth (whatsoever covering an infinite scope), shall be bound in the abode of God as well.

Once more: Jesus said, "And I will give unto thee the keys of the kingdom of heaven: and whatsoever thou shalt bind on earth shall be bound in heaven: and whatsoever thou shalt loose on earth shall be loosed in heaven."

Christ's giving of these keys in the first part of this verse represents the giving of permission, authority and ability to enter into the kingdom of heaven to transact spiritual business. **The remainder of the verse tells the believer how to transact that spiritual business.**

Nearly everyone has heard teachings on binding and loosing, depending upon the church or denomination where you received most of your teaching. The basic teaching I learned illustrated the binding of the devil or evil spirits and the loosing of the Holy Spirit or a ministering spirit to a troubled person or into a troubled situation. I have also heard this Scripture used as a means to "loose" a person from bondage.

I moved in a limited understanding of this, but I did not practice it with much assurance. My main problem was that there is no scriptural record of Jesus ever binding an evil spirit or a demon. He either rebuked them or told them to get out. Binding an evil spirit will restrain or deactivate that spirit's power, but Jesus knew this was not a resolution of the root problem. That would require a different approach. Jesus was more interested in driving evil spirits away. He knew there was a far more beneficial use of binding and loosing.

I began to search for the fullness of the truth of Matthew 16:19 in prayer and from commentaries, lexicons and study books. I initially found that the Greek word for bind, *deo,* means to bind, be in bonds, knit, fasten, tie and wind. This word is related to *deomai,* meaning to beg as in binding oneself to petition, beseech, make request and pray. It is also compared to *dei* and *deon,* basically meaning it is necessary, must, needs, ought and should.

Now what do we do with these word studies? I ask you to do one thing at this point—simply recognize that the word "bind," in its various tenses, is more complex and meaningful than generally thought. It is meant to be used for far more than just tying up an evil spirit.

The Greek word for loose, *luo,* means to loosen, break up, destroy, dissolve, unloose, melt and put off. *Luo* is related to *rhegnumi* and *agnumi* which mean to break, wreck, crack to sunder by separation of its parts, shatter to minute fragments, disrupt, lacerate, convulse, burst, rend and tear. Now those are words a spiritual warrior can get into!

Reconsider the idea of "loosing" the Holy Spirit or a ministering spirit that they might intervene in a situation. What in the world would you possibly loose the Holy

Spirit from, anyway? He's about as free and unfettered as anyone could ever be. What might you really be saying when you loose an individual from his or her bondage?

I didn't really understand the ramifications of these definitions at first, so I took my dilemma to several who taught on spiritual warfare and prayer. I was repeatedly told I didn't understand, I had a wrong interpretation and I was headed for trouble. That did not exactly inspire me to continue along this vein! But I checked and rechecked the references again, prayed about them and it still looked like there was something important there. I could not get anyone else to see it, though. As I was not eager to pursue or promote "wrong doctrine," I finally gave up after two years.

But the thoughts continued to gently simmer in my spirit. In early 1988, the Lord caused me to browse through a book of an internationally known Bible teacher I have always respected. I found he also disagreed with the general interpretation of binding and loosing that I had been taught. I am fully aware this is not the best reason for surrendering to a new revelation, but this was the push I needed. I repented of my doubt and fear of rejection and asked God to enlarge my understanding. I was finally ready to stop seeking understanding from others and listen to Him.

I was ready to seek the whole truth. In the next chapter, I want to talk about how often we fail to search for the whole truth.

SUMMARY

1. Every believer has an equal privilege and is worthy to receive because he or she is in Jesus Christ.
2. God does not desire to withhold any good thing from you. The devil cannot keep any good thing from you. Only you can oppose your receiving.
3. You can stop opposing yourself by stripping off, tearing down and moving out the trappings of your old nature, enlarging your capacity to receive.
4. Every believer comes to Christ with certain mind sets of misinformation. The mind is not instantly renewed at the moment of new birth.
5. Scripturally correct teaching will not automatically clear up wrong ideas. Truth can be twisted if it filters through a mind filled with strongholds.
6. Elijah, the prophet of fire, had at least one wrong mind set and stronghold that caused him to run and hide when the right circumstance played out.
7. Jesus has given us the keys to dealing with those strongholds—they are found in Matthew 16:19 and 18:18.

CHAPTER 2

The Rest of the Truth

Puzzle Pieces

When you first come to Christ, your life is like a pile of jigsaw puzzle pieces. By faith you believe there is a potential for your life to become like the box lid God has in heaven—a pleasing picture to Him and to the others around you. But how all the pieces will fit together is not clear. This mystery is further complicated by your lack of understanding that many of your most cherished pieces won't fit in the final picture.

God has been waiting to help you throw out the wrong pieces and put the right pieces into place. When you accepted Christ as your Lord and Master, you gave the Holy Spirit the green light to start your spiritual engine and begin the process.

Well, of course, you saw the first problem right away. He wanted to remove some of your favorite pieces. You had acquired them, you were familiar with them, they were yours and you were ready to fight to keep them! I did it, too. Aren't we funny creatures?

Undeterred by such preconceived notions when new believers are born into the kingdom of God, the Holy Spirit begins His work anyway. He will usually put the border together for us, giving a godly definition to the boundaries and limits of our lives. And then He finally hands us our first piece to place into the picture. If you were a typical new Christian like me, we grabbed it and hit the ground running.

We tried here and we tried there—going off to try yet again in another spot. Everyone but God was queried about where the piece should go as we pushed it into likely looking areas. Finally we threw it down and cried, "It doesn't fit, God!"

Patiently He said, *"Yes, it does, child, and I've been waiting to show you. It fits perfectly right here."* It was so simple and we knew what to do then! So we immediately reached for the brightest-colored piece in the pile and God said, *"No, not that one. Take this one."*

"I don't want that one, God, it looks boring! I'd rather have the pretty one. Please?" How often we want to reject things God wants to give us because they look uninteresting. We grab for the bright pieces instead, only to find they won't fit anywhere. That does not mean they will never fit, they just won't fit yet.

There is a purpose and an order to the arranging of the pieces in our lives that require certain pieces to be in place first. Many of the biggest, brightest pieces need strong foundational pieces to support them. These foundation pieces include patience, love, submission, restored relationships, jobs, friends, education, the fruit of the Holy Spirit, gain and loss, joy and sorrow, opportunities and waiting. And mixed all through is the mystery factor—those wrong pieces we won't surrender.

And the Holy Spirit continues His work. Just when we begin to think we nearly have our picture completed, God suddenly enlarges our borders. There are new areas to fill and the picture keeps growing.

As a new Christian, I resisted surrendering any but the ugliest of my wrong pieces and I was bored with foundation pieces. The flashy ones looked much better to me. I was pretty stubborn at first, but gradually I learned God won't use you very much if you don't have foundation balance. And I wanted to hear Him say, *"I can channel my power and anointing through you because you have balance. You won't fall over."*

After a few years, my picture seemed in order in most areas. But I had reached a point where the remaining wrong pieces were choking me and it was getting hard to find any "right" pieces. For a season, I couldn't seem to find anything of God at all. Many hours were spent on my knees, ready to do anything if He would only let me find Him again. I was so desperate, I prayed things that caused friends to cringe. "God, do whatever you have to. Crush me, break me, make me willing. I don't care what you do, God, just get it over with."

The Holy Spirit was faithful and some of the things that came out of those prayers were hard to bear. But God answered and my life began to change dramatically.

I began to search the Word to see if what I had been taught was true. This was a very frustrating time, for I was used to being fed truth. Yet something kept nudging me to try and I began to find some amazing gaps in my understanding. Trying to bridge those gaps brought forth a deeper understanding of a pattern of continuity in some of the different interpretations that have split Christians into camps. We tend to concentrate so intensely on the one facet we've been taught, we often miss the bigger picture.

But, let me start at the beginning. I finally settled my relationship with the Lord in Sacramento, California, in the spring of 1973. My early views of Christianity ran parallel to that well-known burger chain jingle where they promised I could "have it my way." I believed God was waiting to take my order, charge it to Jesus' account and deliver the goods with a minimum amount of standing in line on my part.

During that period of time in Christian circles, there was a good deal of well-meant witnessing and discipling based on the promise that once you accepted Jesus, your troubles were over. Become a Christian, be a King's kid and the whole world becomes yours. In the larger scheme of God's overall plan, this is true. But in the dying-to-self process of learning to trust and obey, day by day, spiritual growth can feel pretty rough some times.

Feeling somewhat left out of that elusive King's kids group, I doggedly pursued my relationship with Him anyway. I did it the hardest way possible, though, as I was spiritually malnourished most of the time. I feasted only on teaching I liked, turning up my nose at anything tasting too strong or that chewed too hard. At that time

I was also not interested in getting my own meal, looking instead for what might be available from someone else's "plate." Like a typical baby, I usually swallowed whatever was put in my mouth if it tasted good and smelled spiritual.

Fortunately I attended a strong church that also sustained an excellent Bible school. There was a constant flow of the Word from several sources within this church, in addition to some of the finest Bible teachers and evangelists from around the world. There was so much meat, even the carnal Christians grew spiritually.

Nearly twenty years later, that same fast-food mentality remains alive and well in the body of Christ. Spiritual food that is tasty, easy to chew and delivered quickly is still the diet of choice. There certainly is an abundance of pre-digested teaching readily available for such spiritual snacking. With today's photo-op, sound-bite level of concentration and intolerance for complex details, many seek the latest and fastest way to get blessed.

From one who learned the hard way, such a spiritual diet will not sustain you when your back is to the wall and Satan is reaching for everything you have. As any military person knows, a determined enemy can overwhelm a malnourished soldier who is equipped only with milk, classroom theory and untested weapons. To be a victorious overcomer, you need life-changing, meat-filled, scripturally proven, tried and tested, whole truth girded about your loins.

This is not what you believe because your most spiritual friend or your favorite evangelist told you it is so. This kind of truth is what you believe because the Word of God says it is so. Jesus said, "...If ye continue in my word, then are ye my disciples indeed; and ye shall know the truth, and the truth shall make you free" (John 8:31-32 KJV).

We certainly can profit from what someone else has learned if we are willing to act upon it ourselves. For example, if you have learned about lights and on/off switches, you have surely turned that knowledge into the experience of banishing the dark. You have also probably taught at least one other person how to flip an "on" switch. Many who have learned that basic truth from someone else have gone on to use electricity to run factories, light entire cities and build satellites. These successful people invested their gain from another's knowledge into personal experience that paid great dividends.

You can have all knowledge and still be undone if you have not tried to do anything with it. Wisdom comes from the experience of acting upon knowledge. In the original Greek text, one of the meanings for truth is "having nothing concealed."

You have to handle and act upon truth to see what may yet be concealed from your understanding of it. This doesn't automatically happen by just attending the biggest seminars, viewing the latest videos and reading the newest books. Wisdom comes from truth found and then acted upon and experienced. Ephesians 3:19 (TAB), "That you may really come to know—practically, through experience for yourselves—the love of Christ, which far surpasses mere knowledge without experience...."

When someone else opens up a new understanding for you, it remains a second-hand revelation until you act and experience it first hand. Second-hand revelation generally is accompanied by second-hand faith which can evaporate quicker than water on a hot griddle when you are in deep trouble. The believer in peril who requests "time out" to call someone else to pump up his or her faith will reveal an enemy who plays by no one's rules except his own.

Please don't misunderstand what I am saying. There is nothing wrong with imitating your spiritual elders to enter into new principles and patterns of victory. This is how new Christians often learn about praying, warfare, witnessing and interacting with other believers. But you will only learn about relationship and truth by seeking, experiencing and making room within yourself to receive from Him.

Discover Your Special Plan and Purpose

Our God is a very personal God. He loves you intensely, having made you with a unique potential to bring joy and pleasure to Him in a way no other human being can. Every one of us knows at least one special person who can lift our hearts and bring a smile to our face just by coming near to us. You were created with a unique, spiritual potential to do that same thing by seeking after Him and coming near to Him. He wants you to desire to be fed directly from His table. You are incredibly special to Him.

Years ago, I began to understand that maybe He did have a special plan and a purpose just for me. I glimpsed it only occasionally, but I finally realized no one else knew any more about it than I did. So I got very serious in my prayers and began to seek Him for understanding.

I was surprised and somewhat intimidated by what He began to say. He showed me there were certain things I had been taught that I simply had accepted as single-level truth. I had not yet realized that a truth from Him is like an uncut diamond when we first receive it—vastly valuable and filled with potential—but with its full brilliance not yet revealed. Once it has been cut into different facets and is polished, the diamond becomes far more complex than it was in its original state. Yet the fully-revealed, expertly-cut, final jewel is still pure diamond just as the original rough stone was.

God is willing to reveal the full brilliance of His truth if you have room to receive it. Truth laid open by the Master Jeweler, himself, is as pure as the single truth you first received—but His sparkling, multi-faceted truth is vastly more valuable. Many do not want, or have room to receive, any more than surface understanding. Too often they are like the person who says, "My mind is made up. Don't confuse me with facts." It is a tragedy when the truth is frozen in one dimension within a believer. Truth must be received, believed and acted upon to bring freedom.

Suppose you asked a small child where she lived and she truthfully replied, "In my house." That is a single-layer truth of the child's understanding. Asked what she did in the house, she replied, "Eat and sleep." That would be additional truth that would not negate the original statement.

Then suppose you asked the child if you could come into her house and spend some time with her. Inside, you found there was no furniture and only a thin pad on the floor where she slept. A carton of near-sour milk and some crackers sat in an otherwise empty kitchen. In response to where her parents were, she replied, "They went to a party two days ago and haven't come back yet."

Nothing the child has revealed to this point has negated her first statement, but you have a far greater understanding of that original truth. You have pursued the original truth until several facets were revealed. You are now ready to act upon this fuller understanding to initiate help and deliverance for the child.

The acceptance of truth in its simplest form often leaves much to be learned. This is what happens when we accept someone else's understanding and make it our truth without ever testing or trying it. Their understanding may be the key that opens our desire to know more, but every believer must seek his or her own personal understanding.

Reading the Bible fifty times does not guarantee spiritual wisdom and understanding, unless you turn what you read into experience and relationship. John records Jesus' strong words to the Jews, "You search and investigate and pore over the Scriptures diligently, because you suppose and trust that you have eternal life through them. And these (very Scriptures) testify about Me! And you still are not willing (but refuse) to come to Me, so that you might have life" (John 5:39-40 TAB).

Reading the Bible diligently is not enough. Jesus acknowledged these religious Jews had studied the Scriptures and searched them earnestly, believing eternal life lay within the words. Yet they were missing everything they were supposed to learn and turn into experience—faith and trust and relationship with Jesus.

Experiencing the Word of God

Moving past reading the Word to experiencing it can be likened, with a small flight of imagination, to a textbook teaching on bicycle riding. Such a written teaching may be quite accurate, yet it is only a collection of words until you test it with practical, hands-on experience. You must take what you have read and get on the bicycle, put your feet on the pedals and shove off! It is only then that you will begin to learn how to cooperate with the forward motion of the machine.

You may suffer some falls with cuts and bruises and scrapes. But each time you get back on the bike, believing and trusting that you can turn your knowledge into further action, you become more sure of your experience. And you know what even the world says—once you learn to ride a bike, you never forget how. Many life-giving concepts in the Word become unshakable, powerful, personal truths you will never forget when those concepts become experiential in your life.

Faith does indeed come by hearing the Word, but faith grows by experiencing the Word. Faith and experience turn hope into manifested reality.

Carrying the natural and the spiritual parallel further, let's talk about how we relate to the world around us in our human, mortal state and how this differs from relating to God's truth.

You have communion with God through your spirit. Your body is in touch with the earthly things of the world around you, receiving and responding through the senses of sight, sound, smell, taste and touch. Your soul can be loosely likened to your personality, consisting of your mind, your emotions and your will.

Your body, your soul and your spirit make up who you are—a fearfully and wonderfully made tripartite being. Yet at times these three parts, designed to work smoothly together, seem to run into each other like the Keystone Kops!

Your mind is like a mainframe computer that is constantly gathering information from the world through the terminals of your senses. The mind receives or rejects input according to what it has been pre-programed to receive, analyzing what it does accept to arrive at various conclusions. These conclusions are strongly influenced by what your senses perceive as truth. Unfortunately, your senses can be completely deceived—as anyone knows who has ever watched a magician or a ventriloquist.

Your emotions come into play to flavor your mind's conclusions. Emotions are powerful, God-given spices to enhance your life. These emotional spices add delicious flavor at times, but can overpower at other times. When they are allowed to flow unchecked, they can have an overwhelmingly unpleasant effect. Filled with sensory perception and emotional flavoring, your mind's conclusions are then downloaded to your will for some form of action—fight, flight, fidget or file for later. Sometimes your will authorizes a reaction quite the opposite of what your spirit would advise.

For example, suppose you entered a conference room at work to find it filled with extremely angry people. Having never conquered old patterns of reacting to irrational anger heaped on you as a child, your senses immediately recognized the looks and the tension. Your emotional memories pumped fear into your mind and your will quickly analyzed this input, sending messages over all your circuits to flee.

You exited the important meeting as quickly as possible only to later learn the anger and tension were the result of the uncovering of dishonesty on the part of your boss. You were to be asked to step up and fill this person's position. Because of your irrational action, you were passed over as a bad choice. Had your will been submitted to the will of God and your mind at one with the mind of Christ, you might have waited for the fullness of the truth and become a part of the solution.

To respond wisely to your circumstances, your mind, will and emotions must be submitted to the will of God and the mind of Christ to override erroneous input from your senses and emotions. Anyone who is not surrendered to God's will and the truth will invariably make some very wrong choices. The key to spiritual success is to know how to submit to His will and the fullness of truth and then make right choices.

The best choice you ever made was to accept Jesus Christ as your Savior. Every other choice you make from that point on, <u>even the wrong ones</u>, will ultimately be worked together for good when you are one of those who love God and are called according to His purposes (Rom. 8:28). Wrong choices may slow down your progress, but know that you know this—if you repent and allow the Holy Spirit to teach you by them, you will be back on track and moving forward again. Only with God can you start over more than once with an unblemished, untarnished, 100 percent, still-intact potential...the same potential He has always intended you to fulfill.

Forgiveness, mercy and grace can place your past under the blood. Let go of it and then leave it under there, for heaven's sake! Regardless of what anyone tells you, God's plan and purposes for you are not limited and diminished because you messed up in the past. Your present, your future, your relationship with the Lord and others will only be diminished by your inability to receive God's grace. You are only limited by the choices you make from this minute forward.

Know Your Enemy

You will be intensely battled for that future, for Satan is waging a very personal assault right now to prevent your having it. You are not just some faceless, no-name, little Christian to him. He knows your name, your phone number, your address, your fears and your strongholds, and he customizes his attacks accordingly. But, bless God, the One in you who is greater happens to be the One who chose your name, your phone number and your address before you were ever born! All you need are the keys to dissolving those fears and shattering the strongholds that have given Satan the only edge he's ever had in your life.

Satan is no dummy. He knows full well that those fears and strongholds are his only edge and he's been accessing and attacking your whole being through them to destroy you before you find that out. You've believed you were only protecting yourself and your understanding by the strongholds you built, but you have actually been cooperating with his plans to destroy you.

How does he get you to do this? First of all, you need to understand what a stronghold is. The original Greek word for stronghold is *ochuroma,* which means to fortify by holding safely. To paraphrase Thayer's Greek-English Lexicon, a stronghold is what one uses to fortify and defend a personal belief, idea or opinion against outside opposition. A stronghold is the fortification around and defense of what you believe, especially when you are dead wrong.

If you have believed and bought into a lie, you will fight to protect that belief. The lie might be that you are unloved, unwanted, unnecessary, unsuccessful, unworthy or any of those other ugly un-words. If you've decided the lie must be true, you will erect a stronghold to defend your right to believe it. Repeated attempts by those around you to convince you it is a lie will be viewed as attacks, causing you to reinforce its protective stronghold. Satan knows that and loves it.

Satan is no minor enemy, for Ezekiel 28 tells us he was created perfect and with great wisdom. He made a deadly error of judgment when he challenged God, but he did not lose his superior intelligence when he was thrown out of heaven. He is still far smarter than any of us. As a believer, you are protected by the blood of Jesus Christ and your standing in Him—but if you have built strongholds around unresolved issues in your life, Satan will be on them like steel on a magnet.

He will turn his vast knowledge of your unmet emotional needs, unresolved memories, pain, anger, bitterness, unforgiveness and hidden sin into an arsenal against you. He will trick you and tempt you by circumstances and situations that reinforce your hurt and fear of having these areas exposed to further pain. I absolutely do not believe Satan can read your mind, but I think he has kept exquisite records of your life. He and his demonic pals know exactly how to use that information to bring about predictable responses in you. However, Satan is not the root of your problem. He only uses what already exists.

The Root Problem

The root problem is the vulnerability of a damaged soul and its strongholds. Erected by a wounded soul to keep further pain out, these strongholds keep the pain in. Erected by a wounded soul to protect lies birthed from traumatic experiences, these strongholds keep God's truth out. Satan knows exactly what kind of stronghold you will erect to protect your unmet needs, wounds, fears and humiliating memories. He assigns spirits to access these strongholds and batter your soul further, impacting your entire being.

There are untold numbers of Christian and secular self-help books out on broken families, abusive childhoods, adult children of alcoholics, codependency and other forms of dysfunction. I've read parts of several and others in their entirety. Rarely did I come away from any of these books without having found a few nuggets of information. It hardly seemed necessary to try to add more information to this wealth of written words.

Yet, there is a need. So many Christians have never been able to overcome their troubled pasts to move into the potential of their present. One evangelist rightfully said, "We've all been used and abused in the past, but that's not the problem. The problem is, what are you going to do about it now?" Far too many haven't any idea how to do something constructive about their past, but that is only part of the problem. What is the rest of it?

God's Word says He who is in the believer is greater than he who is in the world. So Satan is not the believer's problem. God's love, promises and faithfulness towards the believer are unchangeable. So God is not the believer's problem. The old nature is the believer's problem. Binding and loosing makes it possible to crucify that old nature and receive God's full healing and restoration.

Many who read this will believe they already understand the truth of binding and loosing in Matthew 16:19 and 18:18. They may have built a stronghold around that belief and reject new facets of the truth. If you identify even slightly with the first sentence of this paragraph, please consider the following paragraph.

Truth can always stand testing. Do not be afraid of finding out you have not had the full truth. You do not have to throw out the truth you have to embrace "new truth." Rather, let me show you how "new truth" may only be additional facets of the very truth you are already standing upon. You may find there is no conflict at all, only deeper understanding.

SUMMARY

1. Learn to seek for all facets of God's truth. It is a tragedy when the truth of God is frozen in one dimension in a believer.
2. We must know the fullness of truth and then act upon it with a surrendered, submitted will to make right choices.
3. Your present and future, your relationship with the Lord and with others will only be diminished by your inability to receive God's grace.
4. Satan knows your name, phone number and address. You are not some faceless, no-name, little Christian to him. But he is not your root problem.
5. The root problem is the vulnerability of a damaged soul and its strongholds erected for protection, yet keeping out only the truth.
6. A stronghold is what you rely upon to fortify, defend and protect your personal beliefs, whether they are right or wrong.
7. There is no need to automatically throw out the truth you understand to embrace "new truth." They may complement each other perfectly.

CHAPTER 3

A New Look at Old Things

New Creatures or Spiritual Accidents?

In my early years as a Christian, I couldn't understand why the Word of God wasn't manifesting itself in power with signs and wonders following my life. I believed, yet feelings of failure and discouragement crept over me again and again. I agonized when I gave up on victory and slipped back into old patterns. Knowing so many others with the same problem, it was hard not to wonder if we really were new creatures or just spiritual accidents.

One such person I knew, a woman I'll call Trudy, had accepted Jesus as her Savior. Having experienced a traumatic relationship with her earthly father, Trudy associated fear and pain with her heavenly Father as well. She had the truth of her spiritual relationship only partially right.

Trudy hung onto Jesus with a fierce tenacity, but she did not trust God or His motives. She saw Him through the emotional baggage of her childhood in an alcoholic home. Her past experience with a father figure convinced her that God would not be there when she needed Him. To hedge against that possibility, she refused to trust Him. She went to church, tithed, read the Bible and prayed to Jesus. She had no intention of giving any more of herself than this.

Many well-meaning Christians tried again and again to assure Trudy she could trust God because He was her Father. Every time they would present this truth, she would experience emotional whiplash. To Trudy, the word "father" meant pain, rejection, humiliation, being unlovable and feeling worthless. To the Christians who stood beside her, the word "Father" meant love, mercy, grace and truth.

Love was a word Trudy had read about in magazines. Trust was a word that meant setting herself up to be disappointed. Mercy was meaningless to her. Truth was what she had already decided to believe. So something always went awry between other Christians' good intentions and Trudy's understanding.

Trudy later told me God revealed that her natural father had been exposed to great trauma in his childhood, but no one had ever tried to help him break out of the bondage of his own pain. She was finally able to see him in a different light and release him from the prison in her mind through forgiveness.

Trudy was repeatedly offered pure truth from the Word of God for years, yet her unresolved pain twisted the truth as it tried to reach her heart. Was her past more powerful than the Word of God? Absolutely not. But consider what happens when you take crystal-clear water and pour it into a dirty filtering system. The clean water will come out polluted and cloudy. There is no fault in the water, the problem is in the unclean filter.

Clogged Filters

Our minds have been used to functioning as filters for everything we have ever heard and experienced. A mind filled with unresolved memories and unmet needs from the past is a mind clogged with pain, and it will cloud and pollute the truth it receives today. The filters of our mental and emotional "receivers" can also become clogged or jammed, just as radar, radios and phone lines can be jammed by an overload of wrong signals. This jamming scrambles the receiving units so that vital information being transmitted perfectly becomes dirty noise—static.

Unmet needs and unresolved memories from yesterday become the source of strongholds protecting distorted ideas, attitudes and patterns of thinking today. It can take a lifetime to overcome these deeply ingrained patterns of thinking if you do not have the keys to tear down the strongholds around them. God's love, mercy and unfailing faithfulness eventually broke through Trudy's mistrust and fear, bringing healing and understanding. But it took far too long for her to stop opposing God and herself and let Him heal her wounds.

Trudy had built strongholds to protect herself from what she perceived as a world not to be trusted. These same strongholds kept her from receiving truth and healing from the Lord, yet allowed Satan access to the wounds and unmet needs from her childhood. How? The lies and pain existed and could be used by the enemy to make Trudy build her walls of distrust and fear higher. Those reinforced walls kept out any new input. She had programed herself to receive only what reinforced what she believed. This allowed Satan to replay her past to mess up her present to destroy her hope for a future.

God's timing is a mystery to us, for His ways are not our ways and His thoughts are not our thoughts (Isa. 55:8-9). Only through the revelation of the Holy Spirit are we ever able to understand what God is doing in us, in others, in the spirit world and in the timing for such works. He will use time to cause our faith to grow, but all too often delay in our lives has no mysterious spiritual meaning at all. Rather, precious, unredeemed time is ticking away while God has to deal with our stubborn wills to get us to let go, strip off and give up our old nature and the strongholds within it.

Doors of Access

Doors of access exist in far too many Christians today. Place yourself in this word picture for a moment. A gang of murderers and thieves are coming up the front walkway to your home. You have superior weapons and you make a stand at your front door, brandishing a laser pistol, an atomic rifle and a space-age shield. The thugs know they cannot take you as you stand there and, at your command, they flee.

What if there are open doors and windows in the back wall of your house? You continue to stand at your front door with your weapons in front of you, full of faith and confidence in your ability to protect yourself. Meanwhile, the murderers and thieves circle around, enter through the back of your home to plunder and pillage your family and wound you, perhaps fatally, from behind your back.

Now let me bring this word picture a little closer to home. The Word of God says, "Submit yourselves, then, to God. Resist the devil, and he will flee from you" (James 4:7 NIV). Suppose you take your stand against the devil and his gang of murderers and thieves as they come up the front walkway of your life. You have on your spiritual armor and you resist them and they flee. Then they circle around to see if you really have it all together and they find your back covered with signs that say:

Stronghold of bitterness: ACCESS HERE ☛
Stronghold of unforgiveness: ACCESS HERE ☛
Stronghold of anger: ACCESS HERE ☛
Stronghold of disbelief: ACCESS HERE ☛
Stronghold of pride: ACCESS HERE ☛

What do you think the enemy is going to do when he flees from before your face? He is going to check you out from every angle to see if you are impenetrable in your stand. If you aren't, God's mercy may save you from a mortal wound, for He desires to protect you from death before your time. But you will take a hit from your enemy, generally a real hard one, so you're not so tempted to try that again.

God is longsuffering with many of your stubborn streaks and strongholds, always working to help you come into the fullness of truth in your relationship with Him. But God will not pardon or condone the sin of the strongholds in your life. Regardless of what cruel and terrible things have been done to you, God will not allow you to hang onto negative feelings and bitterness and still enter the fullness of your inheritance. Such strongholds defile your right standing with God.

Right Standing With God

Soberly consider this verse, "The eyes of the Lord are upon the righteous—those who are upright and in right standing with God—and His ears are attentive to their prayer. But the face of the Lord is against those who practice evil—to oppose them, to frustrate and defeat them" (1 Pet. 3:12 TAB). Thayer's Greek-English Lexicon describes the Greek word translated here as "evil" as universally meaning: of a bad nature; not such as it ought to be; a mode of thinking, feeling or acting that is base, wrong or wicked.

Strongholds not only allow access for demonic torment and torture, they also affect the believer's right standing with the Lord by protecting wrong attitudes, thoughts and feelings. The verse above says He is attentive to the prayers of those who are upright and in right standing with Him. His face is against those who are not in right standing with Him. There is no middle ground—either you are in right standing with Him or you are not.

If you are not, even though you are under the blood and the recipient of His mercy, you can cause Him to oppose, frustrate and defeat you in your prayers. It is the prayers of the one who is in right standing that God hears. James very specifically tells us the earnest prayer of a righteous man is the one that availeth much (James 5:16). It is the righteous man or woman whose communication lines are up and whose strongholds are down who consistently reaches the ear of the Father (1 Pet. 3:12).

In fact, the prayer of one who is in right standing has truly awesome power to impact lives. God "...will even deliver the one (for whom you intercede) who is not innocent; yes, he will be delivered through the cleanness of your hands" (Job 22:30 TAB). We can read in the Book of Job where God put this truth into practice when He was ready to deal with Job's "comforters."

"...I am angry with you and your two friends, because you have not spoken of me what is right...(but) my servant Job will pray for you, and I will accept his prayer and not deal with you according to your folly..." (Job 42:7-8 NIV).

Job was a man considered blameless and upright before God. But when he became discouraged and frustrated over the harsh and cruel circumstances that had come down upon him, God rebuked him with strong words out of the storm of a whirlwind. When Job repented before the Lord for having spoken of things he did not understand, Job reestablished his open lines of communication with God. Then his prayers had the power to deliver those who were not innocent.

Many believers simply do not believe God would oppose or defeat them because of strongholds in their lives. His mercy has spared many in such disbelief and disobedience, but His mercy will not always be extended towards their willfulness. Strongholds are always reinforced when a believer chooses to ignore God's plea to tear them down. It is a vicious cycle that only benefits the enemy.

Strongholds can exist even in those who deeply love the Lord. Some realize they are there, but they've given up on ever destroying them. There are those who only know something is wrong, but they believe it is guilt over having failed. There are those who refuse to admit anything is wrong, denying the reality of their pain and despair. God is a supernatural God. Being honest does not negate His power, nor does it negate His promises. Many Christians equate facing reality with disbelief and doubt. There are times when you have to be painfully realistic to overcome what is keeping you from fulfilling God's plan for your life.

Reconciliation and Restoration Promised

On the brighter side now, the Word says God has committed unto us the ministry and the word of reconciliation (2 Cor. 5:18-19). The Greek word for reconciliation in these verses is *katallage,* meaning exchange or restoration to favor with God. Part of this occurs as we are transformed by the renewing (renovation) of our minds (Rom. 12:2).

Webster's Dictionary says that "renew" means to restore, rebuild, reestablish, renovate. Consider what first happens on the site of any major renovation project. The pigeon and mice droppings have to be shoveled out, the smelly carpet has to be ripped up and the broken plumbing has to be stripped away. The stained walls, sagging ceilings, musty closets and crooked cupboards have to be torn down, broken into pieces and hauled out. Only then can the renewal part of the restoration begin.

The grubby, stinky, stained old things in your mind, will and emotions also have to be shoveled out, torn up, stripped away, broken apart and removed to make room for your renewal to begin.

Think about the woman in Second Kings 4, the widow of the prophet, who was about to lose her two sons into slavery to satisfy her creditors. She had nothing left to her name but a little oil. She cried out to the prophet Elisha for help. Elisha told her to ask all her neighbors for empty jars and then lock herself inside with the jars and her sons and begin to pour the bit of oil into the jars.

Elisha promised it would not stop flowing until all the jars were filled. She would be able to sell the oil, pay off all her debts and live on what was left over. What if that woman had not bothered to clean out any old contents from the jars? The miracle required fully empty jars, jars capable of receiving. Your miracle of receiving from God may be diminished, perhaps completely blocked, because your jars are full of old rubble.

The first miracle Jesus ever performed was the turning of the water into the wine at the wedding in Cana in John 2:7. Jesus told the servants to take jars and fill them to the brim with water which He then turned into wine for the wedding supper. He filled the jars with a miracle. What if those jars had been filled with refuse?

Acts 3:19-21 (TAB) records these words: "So repent—change your mind and purpose; turn around and return (to God), that your sins may be erased (blotted out, wiped clean), that times of refreshing—of recovering from the effects of heat, of reviving with fresh air—may come from the presence of the Lord; and that He may send (to you) the Christ, the Messiah, Who before was designated and appointed for you, Jesus, Whom heaven must receive (and retain) until the time for a complete restoration of all that God spoke by the mouth of all the holy prophets for ages past—from the most ancient times in the memory of man."

We can be refreshed and revived and recover from the effects of previous experiences. As we make room in our souls to receive renewal and restoration, we are even cooperating with the very restoration of all things that will bring about the return of Jesus. God has promised restoration all through His Word.

"Behold, I will send you Elijah the prophet before the great and terrible day of the Lord comes. And he shall turn (and reconcile) the hearts of the (estranged) fathers to the (ungodly) children, and the hearts of the (rebellious) children to (the piety of) their fathers (a reconciliation produced by repentance of the ungodly..." (Mal. 4:5-6 TAB). **Restoration.**

"...After those days, saith the Lord, I will put my law in their inward parts, and write it in their hearts; and will be their God, and they shall be my people" (Jer. 31:33 KJV). **Restoration.**

"And I will restore to you the years that the locust hath eaten, the cankerworm, and the caterpillar, and the palmerworm, my great army which I sent among you. And ye shall eat in plenty, and be satisfied, and praise the name of the Lord your God, that hath dealt wondrously with you: and my people shall never be ashamed" (Joel 2:25-26 KJV). **Restoration.**

"...But be transformed (changed) by the (entire) renewal of your mind—by its new ideals and its new attitude—so that you may prove (for yourselves) what is the good and acceptable and perfect will of God..." (Rom. 12:2 TAB). **Restoration.**

God has always wanted to restore men and women to himself. He sent His Son to die on the cross to bring about a blood-bought way for man to come fully into that restoration. Jesus is now being retained in heaven until this has been fully accomplished. We partake of this restoration by making room to receive it.

Receiving Restoration and Renewal

Everything in the Word of God exhorts us to expect restoration and renewal. But so many Christians aren't receiving and experiencing restoration and renewal or power in these last days. They are too busy trying to defend themselves against the enemy. Who has time to be used in miracles and signs and wonders? Who has time to lead captives free or heal the sick? With the exhaustion from life's grinding pressures, struggling to pay the bills, keeping a roof over their heads and fighting to prevent their families from falling apart—indeed, who has time for such things?

As a believer, you may be desperately caught up in your own fight to keep your head above water. You give yourself to your family, your work, your church and your friends. You may have a kid experimenting with drugs or a parent with a life-threatening disease. As you juggle these things, you try desperately to maintain some kind of a personal balance so you won't slide off in the wrong direction and let them all down.

So, who has time to walk in the Spirit and do what Jesus did, let alone even greater things? Is there really anyone other than Jesus who can? Yes, there is, any believer who has learned to conquer his or her old nature. Any believer can resist the enemy and cause him to flee. Any believer can walk in the power of the Holy Spirit, receive from God and bring about deliverance through the cleanness of their own hands.

"But you just don't know what I've been through..." comes the familiar cry. Yes, I do. I have had struggling Christians share anguished pasts with me, some of them too terrible to repeat here. In the times we live in, it is a rare believer who hasn't experienced some form of extreme trauma.

The proof of your freedom from the effects of your past experiences is evidenced in whether or not the will of God is prospering in your hands today. If it is not, you have inner strongholds causing you to oppose yourself and God. Hell is only able to sustain its program against you when it is not resisted. It is, however, very difficult to resist the enemy if you are like a house or kingdom that is divided—a house that opposes itself.

These last days have brought such an unleashing of evil that the abused person is no longer the exception. Tragically, the person raised in a perfectly normal home is the exception. If you look past the determined smiles on the Sunday faces, you will find the body of Christ is filled with the walking wounded. The world is a mess, time is running out and those who are supposed to have the answers are themselves struggling just to survive. Churches and pastors are overwhelmed with helping their members hold families, finances, homes and shattered hopes together. Jesus keeps offering healing, yet so few seem able to receive it.

Struggling Cannot Bring Renewal

I do understand struggling. I spent more than thirty years struggling before becoming a Christian. I also spent several more years struggling after becoming a Christian, earnestly searching in, copying down and quoting from the Word that I was a new creature. I claimed every promise I could find, even those for certain people during specific time periods in the Old Testament. I didn't care if theologians said I could properly do so or not, I personally claimed every good sounding word I could find! But my past still haunted me when certain circumstances arose.

Some healing and renewal came through the Word, good Christian books, fellowshiping and prayer. Yet I knew there had to be more for God's people, so I set out to find it.

I read in more than one book how we need to allow God to open up our past memories and walk us through them again to relive their outcome and forgive and be healed. I experienced this to some degree, but it didn't seem to bring lasting answers.

Several books insisted that a wounded person needs to confront the one who hurt them. I couldn't see how that tied in with the greatest healing of all—forgiveness. What if confronting would inflict devastation on innocent parties? What if that person had long since died? And I had a real problem with the esoteric suggestion of confronting an empty chair or headstone in a cemetery!

The majority of the books urged those who were wounded to seek counseling and support groups. The reality of today's troubled economy is that few can afford professional counseling for any length of time. Others, through fear or denial, will not approach a support group. Instead, a great many use family members, friends, spiritual leaders, counselors or groups as relief valves to vent just enough pain and pressure to go on. This also enables them to avoid dealing directly with God.

I have read several of the twelve-step program books written for Christians and I see their merit in helping men and women to come out of denial. But rarely do these programs deal with the strongholds that cause people to oppose themselves. I attended one Christian twelve-step group about three years ago to get a better understanding of their function. I was amazed to hear a group leader glowingly describe the sixteen groups she had belonged to. This leader seemed to be a group "groupie."

I attended a second Christian twelve-step meeting in another city several months later, still seeking understanding of the twelve-step phenomena sweeping our nation. The leader repeatedly stressed the necessity of "working the program every day," saying, "I have been working the program for years. Your lifeline is that you can always call someone or go to a meeting when things start to get out of control." I was concerned that a leader who had "worked a program" for nearly a decade would remain so dependent upon it. I am sure the leaders of these groups have the best of intentions, but I question the depth or permanency of healing that comes from such twelve-step programs.

The Bible gives no record of Saul of Tarsus finding a counselor or a support group to overcome the guilt of his treacherous past—nor Peter for his monumental failings—nor Moses for his anger and act of murder—nor David for ensuring that Bathsheba's husband would be killed in battle. Jesus did not send the woman caught in adultery (in John 8) away to find help. She knew she was exposed before Him as she stood there and she submitted herself to the inevitability of whatever He was about to say or do. He simply said, *"There is no one left to condemn you and neither do I. Go and sin no more."*

Beautiful words from the living Word, Jesus Christ. He forgave her of her past and directed her towards her future. He told her she was not condemned by Him, nor was there anyone else with the courage to condemn her in His presence. These words of truth brought her spiritual and emotional freedom. Each one of these Bible personalities received mercy and healing from the Lord.

Healing Comes From Total Surrender

You cannot heal yourself by a strong will to survive or by working a "program." You are healed by surrendering everything in your life—past, present and future—to the will of God and then receiving healing from Him. This can be a fearful thing if you have always managed to avoid dealing directly with God, but there has to come a time when you finally want to be free. If a counselor, program or group has helped you come to this point, then they have served you well. But they cannot heal you. The only way to be truly free is to strip your old nature of everything it derives power from, tear down the strongholds you have erected and then allow God to spiritually realign your life.

Understanding Strongholds

Your strongholds may have actually enabled you to survive terrifying circumstances in your past that were out of your control. This is one of the reasons you trust them. But if they are still in place in your life, they are providing access for the enemy's assaults. They are also protecting wrong attitudes, beliefs and patterns of thought you have learned to trust more than you trust the truth.

We build the strongholds, we rely on them to protect us and we fight like crazy to keep them. Strongholds and what they protect often cross and overlap the categories of wrong attitudes, patterns of thinking, beliefs, etc., which will be discussed later. That is not important—what is important is to tear them apart and take them down, whatever their name.

As you read the following list, remember that a stronghold is what we rely upon to defend and protect our right to believe something. Here are a few of the strongholds we build:

- **Suspicion**: Being painfully deceived can cause the building of a stronghold of suspicion to protect against being deceived again. This stronghold will resist intimacy with God.

•**Doubt**: The stronghold of doubt is usually one of the most obvious strongholds. It frequently accompanies a stronghold of suspicion which can masquerade so well, its existence is often totally denied.

• **Independence**: Rejection can cause the building of a stronghold of independence and self-sufficiency around pain, fortifying a right to never be vulnerable again. This can include any vulnerability to the work of the Holy Spirit.

• **False Security**: When unmet needs exist, a stronghold of false security may be erected. This stronghold projects a facade of great strength intended to keep others from knowing how internally fragile and needy a person is. This can extend to keeping God at arm's length, as well.

• **Confusion**: A stronghold of confusion is erected by the old nature to mask the true understanding of a given issue or many issues. This stronghold leads to discouragement and depression (which can be strongholds, too).

• **Unforgiveness:** When someone has been abused or deeply hurt, unless forgiveness and healing come, strongholds of unforgiveness, bitterness or anger are erected to justify the role of being a victim.

• **Distrust**: Betrayal can cause the building of a stronghold of distrust to prevent anyone from getting close enough to betray again. This person will generally also be unable to fully trust God whose perfect love casts out fear.

- **Control and Manipulation**: A childhood filled with chaos, instability and everything seemingly out of control can build a stronghold of control to prevent ever being at the mercy of another again.
- **Self-Indulgence**: This stronghold is built to justify and protect the right to indulge self to compensate for unmet needs and pain. This stronghold also justifies a right to chemically alter reality with drugs or alcohol to blot out pain.
- **Fear**: Fear is a common, but slightly different stronghold. People generally do not build this stronghold for protection, rather it is erected around great apprehension and anxiety over unresolved experiences and memories.
- **Denial**: A stronghold of denial refuses to acknowledge any of the above things. Denial is a valid, temporary mental and emotional coping mechanism to enable the human mind to survive certain traumatic situations—similar to how shock shuts down and prevents a severely wounded body from death. Denial enables abused children to survive unbearable situations. But just as shock becomes dangerous and life-threatening when a person cannot come out of it, so does denial when it becomes a stronghold.

These are some of the strongholds we erect around things we cannot bear to face. You can loose the grip of every one of them and what they are protecting in your life and the lives of others, thereby making room for that which is right and healing. The binding and loosing that accomplishes this is ours by the grace of God and the power of the resurrected Lord Jesus Christ.

We have to choose to make room to receive the renewal and restoration that will replace old things. God generally will not forcibly take what you don't want to surrender. The excuse, "If God wants me to give it up, He'll take it from me," is old-nature whitewash hogwash!

Those who bind and loose don't become super-Christians, self-empowered to leap tall strongholds in a single bound. Those who bind and loose just use their keys to the kingdom. Jesus made it possible for us to have His support, the Holy Spirit's comfort, access to the Father's love and these keys to overcome our old natures. But He will not force us to accept His help. We are our strongest when we realize we need His help for everything, from our breathing to our believing.

Are you aware that what you have learned to believe about yourself can be more powerful in shaping your life than the truth? You need His help in sorting through your beliefs to make room for the truth. Then you need to sort through the bits and pieces of truth you have and let God help you focus them into powerful, right beliefs. That process is somewhat like turning a handful of loose buckshot into a twelve-gauge shotgun shell.

SUMMARY

1. Many use family members, friends, spiritual leaders, counselors or groups as relief valves to vent just enough pain and pressure to enable them to go on.
2. Your strongholds may have enabled you to survive terrifying circumstances in your past that were out of your control. This is why you trust them.
3. Becoming new creatures in Christ is a process the devil fights with everything he can and the old nature helps him.
4. A mind filled with unresolved pain and unmet needs will distort everything that filters through it. Many program themselves to receive only what reinforces what they already believe.
5. The proof of your freedom from your past is evidenced in whether or not the will of God is prospering in your hands.
6. Hell is only able to sustain its program against you if it is not resisted. It is difficult to resist when you are divided and opposing yourself.
7. What you believe about yourself can be more powerful in shaping your future than the truth.

CHAPTER 4

Binding

Two Kinds of Binding

When I finally submitted to this new understanding, the Lord began to show me the two sides to binding. There is a binding which imprisons and chains and there is a wonderful, helpful binding. In the Old Testament, the positive side of binding is shown in the word *qashar* which means to tie, gird, confine, compact, bind, conspire, join together, knit. This is the same Hebrew word used in the following Scriptures referring to the value of God's wisdom and truth:

"Let not mercy and truth forsake thee: **bind** them about thy neck; write them upon the table of thine heart" (Prov. 3:3 KJV).

"**Bind** them (your father's God-given commandments—TAB) continually upon thine heart, and tie them about thy neck" (Prov. 6:21 KJV).

"**Bind** them upon thy fingers, write them upon the table of thine heart" (Prov. 7:3 KJV).

There is a good example of both sides of binding in Isaiah 61:1 (KJV), "The Spirit of the Lord God is upon me; because the Lord hath anointed me to preach good tidings unto the meek; he hath sent me to **bind** up the brokenhearted, to proclaim liberty to the captives, and the opening of the prison to them that are **bound**."

The Hebrew word *chabash* as used here for **bind** means heal, **bind** up, wrap about and hold together. We read within the very same Scripture that spiritual prison doors are to be opened to set free those the enemy has **bound** (Hebrew: *'acar*), made prisoner, held fast, girded about, kept.

So many people see only the one side of binding, having firmly connected the act with a mental image of chaining up something so it can't hurt them. I faced the closed door of this mental image again and again as I tried to present the idea of a positive side of binding. Finally, I asked God for a word picture such as Jesus used in the parables to communicate this positive side.

At once I began to picture a parent binding a baby to their body with a cloth baby-wrap as was used in the sixties and seventies. When that little one was bound to the parent, wherever the parent went, the baby went. The baby had a distinct personality and thoughts of its own, but it was bound to and experiencing the wiser, more mature will of the parent. If the parent went into sunshine and warmth, the baby went into sunshine and warmth. If the parent came into the presence of a sweet scent or a pleasant sound, the baby smelled that same sweet scent and heard the same sound. When the parent avoided dangerous situations, the baby avoided danger.

For all intents and purposes, the baby became as one with the parent even though it was still an individual entity. This idea was very exciting, if still a little fuzzy, but I decided to act on it! At first I couldn't decide what to bind to what. But, as the wobbly one in my relationship with the Father, I was like the baby in the word picture. Since the things of God are constant, it only made sense to bind myself to the steadfast things of God.

So I began by binding my will, my thoughts and my life to the will of God. I bound my days and nights, the work of my hands and everything I could think of to the will of God, all in the name of Jesus Christ. I use the name of Jesus in all my prayers. Doing so gives me a sense of finally belonging to the real "in crowd" when I ask for things in Jesus' all-powerful name.

As I worked with this simplest form of binding myself to something of God, I began to feel a gentle steadying throughout my day. I had a sense of lining up with God's will more than I ever had before with a new balance and sure-footedness in my spiritual walk. The Father can easily negotiate the narrowest, trickiest, most dangerous pathway. Bound to His will, I felt secure in walking where I would never have been able to negotiate on my own.

I didn't realize it at the time, but I was aligning myself with the words of Christ as He prayed, "Our Father in heaven, hallowed be your name, your kingdom come, your will be done, on earth as it is heaven" (Matt. 6:9-10 NIV). I was ensuring my will's cooperation on earth with His will in heaven by the words of my mouth (Matt. 16:19 and 18:18).

Next I decided to bind myself to the truth of God. Deception rarely comes at the child of God in pure black. More often than not, it comes in degrees of off-white and pale grey that can be misinterpreted by humans. At that point, it seemed prudent to back up binding myself to the truth of God with loosing (smashing, crushing, destroying, disrupting, lacerating, etc.) any deception from the enemy—sort of the double-barreled shotgun approach.

Right away I began to sense a new awareness of missing pieces in situations. It took time, but I was focusing in on what the Holy Spirit was showing me. I was receiving new spiritual insight from the Holy Spirit with regard to others' hidden agendas, unseen feelings and motivations. I began to sense facades people had erected to cover up hurt or feelings of inadequacy. I became more sensitive instead of reacting to their words and walls.

Amazed at what was happening, I searched further for things to bind myself to. God's will and the truth and the blood are all immutable and ever constant. Everything about God—every attribute, every basic spiritual component of His love and provision for us—is stable, trustworthy and always there. I'm the one in our relationship who has a tendency to waver and wander off, so it's me who needs to be fully aware of His attributes.

On my own, filled with the cares of the world and my life, I can forget the power of the blood of Jesus Christ. I don't always remember that the blood can cleanse my conscience from dead works. So I began to bind myself to an awareness of the blood of Jesus, its healing power, its protection, its covering and its cleansing. I still do this today and it always makes me feel covered, protected, privileged, loved and scrubbed after a hard day in the world.

I was on a spiritual roll! Although my understanding was still slightly fuzzy, I was making contact with things in the Word of God that had eluded me up to that point.

A Strengthened and Steadied Mind

I do not know if I am a writer because of my active imagination or if I have an active imagination because I write, but I have an internal VCR that is always set on PLAY. At night I dream vivid dreams and during most of my waking hours, I can look inward and watch pictures and thoughts passing by. Sometimes it will be words of a manuscript or dialogue from a play or skit I'm thinking about. Other times it will simply be pictures or recalled memories.

This was very entertaining in my younger days as I was an only child and spent a great deal of time alone. As I grew older, it became more of a problem as my unrenewed mind began to rerun embarrassing and humiliating memories I did not want to remember. These memories were harsh flashbacks of cruel words, times of rejection and other painful things. I began to allow my mind to rewrite the situations with biting putdowns and comebacks from me. They were meant to exist only inside my mind, yet once composed, the sharp words seemed to pop out of my mouth at the first provocation.

This was something I would struggle with most of my life—rehearsing my hurts and getting even in my mind, then finding the words spilling out of my mouth when I was under pressure. It didn't stop after I became a Christian.

I battled against such thought patterns because of a desire to conform to the image of Christ. Knowing I needed to take my thoughts captive to Jesus, I began to bind my mind to the mind of Christ. I knew the Word in Philippians 2:5 (KJV), "Let this mind be in you, which was also in Christ Jesus," and in First Corinthians 2:16, "...but we have the mind of Christ." I felt sure that binding my mind to the mind of Christ would help me line up with Second Corinthians 10:5 (KJV), "Casting down imaginations, and every high thing that exalteth itself against the knowledge of God, and bringing into captivity every thought to the obedience of Christ."

It worked! I began to instantly recognize when my thoughts were slipping out of line and I knew I could choose to stop them. Making that choice was harder, but the constant binding of my will to the will of God steadied, strengthened and finally brought me into consistent victory. When I concentrated on binding my mind to Christ's mind and the truth, my old patterns of thinking would back off. I wasn't sure what to do about all of the old thoughts yet, but I could feel a constraint upon them for the first time in my life.

Other benefits began to manifest themselves. For many years, I've done consulting and trouble-shooting in a variety of office situations, constantly adjusting to new people and situations that no one else knew how or cared to handle. One of the strangest jobs I landed in was the physical organization and computerization of an electronic filing system for a chemical engineering resource library. It isn't easy to even say that, let alone do it!

I received this particular project because I had writing experience. I can only surmise they related writing books with libraries or something like that. I was given a portable computer and shown an empty library filled with piles of reference magazines and boxes of technical books with titles I could barely pronounce. The instructions were to "have at it." I had no chemical or engineering understanding, only a sudden desire to be somewhere else. I had very little to go on as to how to achieve the desired end result.

At this point in my life, I was already moving in binding and loosing prayers. I sat down on the floor of that library in the middle of all those boxes and piles and bound my mind to the mind of Christ while claiming the Word that says I could do all things through Jesus Christ who strengthened me—over and over and over. I did this with my eyes closed, my head bowed and my back to the door, hoping to give the appearance of studying the books in my lap. My eyes were closed as it was too depressing to look at the jumbled stacks around me. My back was to the door to avoid the questioning looks on the hopeful faces which occasionally peeked around the door post.

As I prayed, my mind began to formulate a logical way to categorize these "foreign" titles. I believe Christ's mind, by the Holy Spirit, was feeding supernatural input into my mind. That beginning quickly progressed into a successful completion of a corporate-level research library. In the natural, there was no way I could have organized all of that material which might as well have been entitled in Russian.

Another word meaning bind also means to compact (*sumbiazo* in the Greek) as used in Ephesians 4:16 (KJV), "From whom (Christ) the whole body fitly joined together and compacted (bound together) by that which every joint supplieth, according to the effectual working in the measure of every part, maketh increase of the body unto the edifying of itself in love."

<u>Thayer's Greek-English Lexicon</u> describes compacted as used here as "to cause to coalesce, to join together, put together into one whole." What a beautiful and very practical word for our daily circumstances. I know the Holy Spirit certainly caused my "library dilemma" to coalesce and come together as I bound my mind to the mind of Jesus Christ.

I realized from that point on that binding my mind to Christ's mind was a powerful key in situations where I did not know how to meet either the revealed or the hidden expectations of others. I used that key to activate the process of being strengthened by Him in situation after situation. I also found I was recognizing truth and getting understanding in many situations that was simply not discernible in the natural. I knew something incredible was beginning to happen in my life.

911 Emergency

Not too long after that I had a very unusual experience that I also attribute to binding my mind to Christ's mind and my will to God's will. I had flown to another city to do some interviews and someone insisted an evangelist tell me her story about "911." Living in a neighborhood that is considered to be somewhat less than safe, this woman was cautious about opening her front door under the best of circumstances. Then one night a man's voice insisted she open the door at once for the police. She refused. Through the peephole in her door, she saw what could be a badge, but she was not certain it was. As she argued with them, the men informed her they were about to break down the door.

She ran to the phone, dialed 911 and reported the scenario. To her surprise, the operator informed her the police were indeed at her door and they certainly would break it down if she did not let them in at once. When she did, the police entered and soon realized they had made a mistake. They apologized and left.

The evangelist sought the Lord and received a wonderful message about the world's natural 911 and the believer's spiritual 91:1, "He who dwells in the secret place of the Most High shall remain stable and fixed under the shadow of the Almighty (Whose power no foe can withstand)" (Ps. 91:1 TAB).

I tingled all over as this evangelist shared her testimony. After flying home, I repeated the story to anyone who would listen. Others found the story interesting, but no one seemed to feel like I did. I even repeated the testimony in my church on the following Sunday night. Everyone was blessed, but again, no one seemed to be particularly impacted but me.

Four nights later, I was startled awake at 3:00 in the morning by a loud pounding on my front door. I was living alone at the time and this was not my favorite night noise. I called out, "Who is it?"

The reply came, "Open the door; it's the police."

I quickly looked through the peephole and saw total darkness. Assuming someone had their finger over the peephole, I said, "Get your finger off the peephole! I'm not opening this door until I can see you."

A male voice whispered loudly, "We had to remove your porch light for cover. Open the door, this is a life-and-death situation."

"I don't know who you are and I'm not opening the door!"

A small light clicked on to shine upon something that might have been a badge, but I couldn't be sure. But in its limited reflection, I could see what appeared to be several black ski masks. I yelled through the door, "I can't tell what that says and you don't look like policemen. I'm not opening this door!"

An urgent male voice quickly replied, "That's because we're SERT officers (Special Emergency Response Team, I would learn later). This is a life-and-death situation. Please open the door!"

Sometimes I am a little slow, but finally I began to realize I had heard everything that was being said once before—in fact, quite recently! "911!" I yelled. "I'm going to call 911."

A muffled voice came back through the door, "Please do, ma'am."

I ran across the living room to punch 911 into my telephone, all the while quoting my spiritual 91:1, "I dwell and abide under the shadow of the Almighty. Thank you, Jesus!" I was quickly informed by the 911 operator that it was indeed a SERT at my front door and it was a life-and-death situation. I returned to the door and threw it open to have five, faceless SERT officers stream into my living room. They were completely outfitted in black from their full coverage masks to their boots. These strange figures carried bullet-proof riot shields, what appeared to be sawed-off shotguns and black two-way radios.

Completely "stable and fixed" (Ps. 91:1 TAB), a fact I did not realize as remarkably unusual until much later, I asked, "What's going on?"

One team member tersely informed me an armed robber was hiding in the house immediately adjacent to mine. My house was needed for the SERT officers and police negotiators to access my back yard to use their bullhorns to convince the armed man to come out and surrender. "Really? What do you want me to do?" I asked.

The leader said, "We'll have everything fully covered. We want you to stay on the other side of your house. I don't suppose you could just go back to bed, could you?"

"You're kidding, right?" I said, laughing.

When he then told me that my front door and side door would have to remain open for their access, I stopped laughing and indicated a concern that the robber might come in one of the open doors. The leader said,

"You don't have to worry about anyone getting in your house, ma'am, just look out any of your windows."

When I did, I was surprised to see my house was surrounded with men in camouflage suits training rifles on the house in question. So I heated some instant coffee in the microwave and went back to my bedroom to read my Bible and pray for everyone involved. Instead of a terror-filled experience, the Lord had prepared me, stabilized me and was about to use me in a unique opportunity. Before I was finally allowed to leave my home nearly nine hours later, I was telephoned by a local radio station and interviewed, on the air live, giving a brief testimony about what had preceded my involvement in the current situation. Thousands of people getting ready for work or driving on the freeway that morning heard the natural and the spiritual "911" testimony.

Prior to having acquired this new stability and ability to see God's hand in everything I walk into, I can't even imagine how I would have reacted. Now really, just think about it. I was alone in my house with hooded, faceless men at my front door demanding entrance to my home at 3:00 in the morning after they had just deactivated my porch light. I'm not sure about you, but that is not my normal, early-morning routine.

Partaking

The positive side of binding is filled with great potential. For instance, think again for a moment about the baby who is bound to its parent. That baby is, for all intents and purposes, one with its stronger and wiser parent. Whatever the parent does, wherever the parent goes, whatever the parent is exposed to...so goes the baby. The baby partakes of the same experiences. Consider this:

> "For we are made partakers of Christ, if we hold the beginning of our confidence stedfast unto the end" (Heb. 3:14 KJV).

> "For they verily for a few days chastened us after their own pleasure; but he (the Lord) for our profit, that we might be partakers of his holiness" (Heb. 12:10 KJV).

> "Whereby are given unto us exceeding great and precious promises; that by these ye might be partakers of the divine nature, having escaped the corruption that is in the world through lust" (2 Pet. 1:4 KJV).

Have you ever wondered how partaking actually occurs? The Greek word translated as partaker means participant, associate, companion, fellowship. As I bind myself to the truth, and to God's will for my life, I am a participant in the Father's will which has always been the will of the Son. My will comes together and begins to coalesce with His will. When God says, *"Let's go this way now,"* I go. When God says, *"Believe I'm going to protect you,"* I become steady and fixed. I feel association and companionship when I bind myself to Christ's mind. I have fellowship as I partake of His thoughts.

Whenever the world is spinning too fast and life is starting to get a little crazy, I stop and reuse my keys to the kingdom—sometimes several times a day in those particularly intense days we all experience. It has never failed that the peace from above always drops gently over me like a feather-soft blanket. I drink in and partake of all He has to share with me.

As I bind myself to the blood of Jesus and the work of the cross, I feel fellowship with Him and His sufferings. I find myself very aware of the miracle-working power of restoration and forgiveness and healing in His blood as it works in my life. I partake of the things of Christ, His holiness, His joy, His peace and His nature. I partake of His presence.

I would almost like to stop right here and stay with that thought, because the next point may cause doctrinal whiplash. If any such injury occurs, call my Counselor at either 91:1 or 1-800-THE-KING.

Dealing With Evil Spirits

There is only one instance in which I bind evil. I do not bind individual spirits such as the spirit of lust, the spirit of lying, the spirit of poverty, etc. I am aware of the doctrines of the importance of naming and speaking directly to these evil spirits, powers, principalities and rulers of darkness. However, I do not find any scriptural reference to Jesus or any of His disciples specifically instructing us to name and bind these spirits. Jesus and His disciples rebuked them as unclean or foul and commanded them to leave.

I do not deny the existence of these spirits. I have seen them manifested and known which spirits they were. I have spoken in the name of Jesus and rebuked them, commanding them to go. Sometimes they did, sometimes they didn't. At the time, I did not recognize why. Now I do. I believe evil and demonic spirits exist, I just don't believe I have to deal with them in the manner generally taught.

There are basically three kinds of spirits we have to deal with: the Holy Spirit, evil spirits and human spirits. The Word of God calls angels ministering spirits, but we do not deal with angels. Rather, God sends them to minister to, war for and deal with us.

In the nearly twenty years I have been a Christian, I have seen much confusion over the issue of the effects of the works of spirits. All too often believers blame whatever appears to be wrong on Satan or one of his evil spirits. Lack of discernment of spirits can cause believers to deny their own culpability in a situation. It is a real temptation to believe an evil spirit has entered into a situation rather than acknowledging a manifestation of ugliness from our own human spirit or old nature. Satan loves to help us believe this.

Even more frightening is when a believer fights a work of the Holy Spirit, believing they are being withstood from their intended goals by Satan. This is a very dangerous error. I am sure God's grace has kept untold numbers of Christians from grieving the Holy Spirit by doing just this.

Evil spirits do exist, working through people to accomplish their goals and they do have the ability to wreak great havoc in human lives. You can bind them with the imprisoning side of binding, but you will just find yourself continuing to bind spirit after spirit if the real problem is not dealt with. Rather than battling such multiple onslaughts, consider how an evil spirit attacks a person in the first place. What do these evil spirits access?

They access the strongholds protecting wrong attitudes, patterns of thinking and beliefs. These strongholds create the spiritual vulnerability in the human soul that evil spirits can access. When you bind evil spirits in the name of Jesus Christ, you can deactivate their power and this is necessary in some circumstances. But if the source of vulnerability in the human soul is not dealt with, it will be accessed by another like spirit and the person will be in the same situation as before.

Have you ever wondered why one person, and not another, seems to be continually vulnerable to spiritual attack in the same manner? That individual has a vulnerability to a particular kind of spirit because of the strongholds in his or her life. A lying spirit will sniff out a stronghold protecting deceptions quicker than a bird dog. A spirit of hate can find a stronghold of anger from clear across town. Satan will constantly lead an individual into situations and circumstances that will put them around such like spirits.

The person who is inordinately sensitive and has built a stronghold around a damaged sense of self-worth will constantly be harassed by a spirit of pride. A person who has been taught to believe they are sickly and weak will build a stronghold to protect that belief. That stronghold will attract a spirit of infirmity which will find easy access to inflict illness and distress upon this person, reinforcing his or her wrong belief. It is a vicious cycle. The permanent answer lies not in binding the evil spirit, but in dealing with the stronghold in the individual that gives such a spirit access and entrance to assault the soul.

By adding the principles of this truth to your prayer life, you will find yourself better equipped to discern individual spirits as they come against you or another person. You will know whether to rebuke the spirit openly or to begin to intercede and destroy strongholds through prayer. In some cases, there is little ground gained by rebuking a spirit and commanding it to go until the stronghold and what it protects has been torn down and destroyed. If this has not been accomplished, a like spirit will immediately reestablish access and intensify its attack on the individual. The doorway of access must be destroyed.

I do not believe Christians can be demon-possessed. But I definitely believe that strongholds create open doors in believers, giving evil spirits access to torment their souls and bodies, thereby distressing their spirits as well. This is not the same thing as possession.

But here is the good part! The tearing down or the destruction of a stronghold in a person's soul closes that point of vulnerability and access. This can be accomplished even in another person, <u>regardless</u> of whether the person in question is willing to cooperate or absolutely refuses help. This is discussed at length in a later chapter.

There is far more to be said on how to deal with these spirits as you discern them or they manifest themselves to you, but that is not the subject at hand. Simply know that if you are always "prayed up," walking in His will and filled daily with His Word, the Holy Spirit will direct your words and actions. He may have you enter into intercession. He may have you anoint with oil and lay hands on someone. Or He may use you in an act of deliverance. If you are bound to the will and purposes of the Father with no doors of access open in your own soul, you will be used to bring victory.

Binding the Strong Man

Jesus does make one reference to binding evil. You can find the same basic reference in Matthew 12 and Mark 3 where He speaks of binding the strong man. A very similar reference occurs in Luke 11. Matthew records Jesus' reply to the Pharisees who accused Him of casting out devils by Beelzebub, the prince of devils, "...But if I cast out devils by the Spirit of God, then the kingdom of God is come unto you. Or else how can one enter into a strong man's house, and spoil his goods, except he first bind the strong man? And then he will spoil his house" (Matt. 12:28-29 KJV).

Verse 29 in the New International Version reads, "...How can anyone enter a strong man's house and carry off his possessions unless he first ties up the strong man? Then he can rob his house."

Luke 11:21-22 (KJV) says, "But if I with the finger of God cast out devils, no doubt the kingdom of God is come unto you. When a strong man armed keepeth his palace, his goods are in peace: But when a stronger than he shall come upon him, and overcome him, he taketh from him all his armour wherein he trusted, and divideth his spoils."

I do not read anywhere in my Bible that I can imprison, permanently chain up or actually destroy Satan. Yet many, myself included, have tried to do just that for years. If the thousands of Christians who have tried to bind Satan in chains according to their understanding of Matthew 16:19 and 18:18 had been successful, he wouldn't still be running loose, now would he? That right is reserved for the Lord and the angel who will cast Satan into the bottomless pit and shut him up for a thousand years.

Christians have been binding Satan for years, over and over and over, and he is still going about as a roaring lion. But the above verses, referring to binding the strong man, obviously do imply an ability to restrain him from preventing us from reclaiming, recovering and restoring that which he has looted and stolen from God's people. The order here would be to first bind the strong man; second, loose his hold upon your stolen possessions (spiritual or natural); and, third, make sure you have made room to receive the restoration of them back to you. These words can help you bind the strong man so he cannot prevent your loosing of his hold upon what is rightfully yours.

As a Christian, you can expose Satan's workings and rebuke him by using the name of Jesus and the Word of God against him, commanding him to flee. Both actions of faith have full power to color him gone from a given situation. The power in the Word of God and the name of Jesus is quite enough to destroy Satan as well, but that final act awaits God's timetable.

But, back to the fact that the Word of God does say that by binding the strong man, we can then take back the spoils of his house. Isaiah 53:12 (KJV) tells us God says this about Jesus, "Therefore will I divide him a portion with the great and he shall divide the spoil with the strong; because he hath poured out his soul unto death: and he was numbered with the transgressors; and he bare the sin of many, and made intercession for the transgressors."

This is related to Luke 11:22 (KJV) which tells us, "But when a stronger (Jesus Christ) than he (Satan) shall come upon him, and overcome him, he taketh from him all his armour wherein he trusted, and divideth his spoils." "Divide" (or divideth), as used here, comes from the Greek word *diadidomai* which means to give throughout a crowd; to distribute or deal out; to deliver over to a successor. The word "spoils" (Greek: *skulon*) as used here means booty.

Jesus in us is stronger than he who is in the world. Jesus has overcome Satan and taken his armor from him. In Christ, we have been given the authority to bind the strong man and impair his ability to prevent us from plundering his house and distributing his spoils back to those who were robbed in the first place.

Jesus said we would do such things in John 14:12-14 (KJV), "Verily, verily, I say unto you, He that believeth on me, the works that I do shall he do also; and greater works than these shall he do; because I go unto my Father. And whatsoever ye shall ask in my name, that will I do, that the Father may be glorified in the Son. If ye shall ask any thing in my name, I will do it."

Old Testament Confirmation

There is an Old Testament confirmation that speaks of the deliverance of captives and prey from Satan's kingdom or house. Isaiah 49:25 (KJV) tells us the Lord says, "...Even the captives of the mighty shall be taken away, and the prey of the terrible shall be delivered: for I will contend with him that contendeth with thee, and I will save thy children." The Hebrew word interpreted as mighty is *gibbor,* meaning powerful, warrior, tyrant and also strong man. The Hebrew word interpreted as terrible is *arits,* meaning fearful, powerful, tyrannical, mighty, oppressor, strong, terrible, violent.

Every thing and every one that Satan has laid claim to has been taken from God's creation, mankind. Jesus has given us instructions on how to render the works of the enemy useless and take the stolen goods and captives back. "...For this purpose the Son of God was manifested, that he might destroy the works of the devil" (1 John 3:8 KJV).

SUMMARY

1. Every attribute of God is stable. We're the ones who waver and wander, so it's us who need to be bound to and aware of His attributes.
2. Rehearsing your hurts and getting even in your mind creates words that spill out when under pressure.
3. When you bind your mind to Christ's mind and the truth, old patterns of thinking back off.
4. Bind also means compacted as in "to cause to coalesce, to join together, put together into one whole."
5. Binding evil spirits can deactivate their power, but it is only a front-line, temporary measure.
6. The permanent answer lies in dealing with the stronghold in the individual that gives the spirit access and entrance to assault that person's soul.
7. You can bind the strong man (Satan), loose his hold upon stolen possessions (spiritual or natural) and receive the restoration of them back to you.

CHAPTER 5

Loosing

Demolishing Strongholds and Bondages

I have never felt more power to impact strongholds and bondages of the enemy than I have felt since I began to sense the truth of loosing. I moved in this understanding rather tentatively at first, but as I realized what was happening, I felt increasingly confident and dangerous. I was turning spiritual understanding into experience!

I began by loosing and destroying what I perceived to be bridges. In my mind I pictured spiritual bridges the enemy and his demons traveled on to drag pain and humiliation from my past into my present. So I loosed the works of Satan, his demons, his influences and these "bridges." At times I felt led to speak the more graphic words of dissolving, destroying, crushing, shattering, breaking apart and melting. That was even more fun! But whether I was loosing or dissolving and destroying, it had the same effect—things began to come down.

These were my beginning efforts to loose destructive things from my life. An interesting point is the fact that I was only partly right about what I was doing, for the enemy had not built "bridges" from my past. Yet my binding and loosing was still having a powerful effect upon his plans to ruin my life.

This brings to mind one special young woman named Sherry who has been a Christian for some time. One of her friends, who had been attending my teaching classes on binding and loosing in early 1992, began praying these principles for Sherry. This friend tried to share some of the teachings with Sherry, stating that she had been praying regularly for Sherry this way. Fearing that some form of hidden mind control was involved in the principle, Sherry demanded that the friend stop praying that way for her. The friend agreed to stop, but asked Sherry to at least just think about what she had said.

Sherry could not seem to forget what the friend had shared and finally decided to try binding something non-human to the things of God (an unusual idea I had not thought of). She was amazed at the results of her prayers. Intrigued, she finally came to a class. As I welcomed her to the meeting, Sherry blurted out defiantly, "I just do the binding. I don't do loosing!" I assured her that was just fine.

I found out later that Sherry didn't even believe in some of the binding principles. But the parts she did believe in, she was using to bind some rather unusual things to the things of God. She bound a desk purchased at a yard sale to the will of God because her young daughter seemed afraid of the desk. Soon the preschooler was happily coloring while sitting at the desk.

Then Sherry finally moved into applying binding principles to humans. She began with a clerk (in a store where one definitely feels constrained to tightly clutch one's purse or wallet) who denied he had shorted her by $10 in change. Frustrated, Sherry left her phone number and went home to spend the afternoon binding him to the mind of Christ. The clerk telephoned later that day and told her that he had found her $10 and to please come and get it. I chuckle every time I think about that young man walking around all afternoon with the thoughts of Jesus Christ bombarding his mind.

Sherry has been binding and loosing with wonderful answers. She bound neighbors who were attending a cultic church to the truth, the will of God and the mind of Christ. Within a very short period of time, the neighbors moved to a good, Bible-based church.

Sherry bound a pastor's daughter to the will and purposes of God, a young girl who was quite ill and whose extensive medical tests had proved to be inconclusive. Sherry was later informed this girl had suddenly just gotten better right after Sherry began to pray for her.

Those in the classes were treated to two months of testimonies of wonderful answers to her prayers of binding. Then, to my amazement, I learned Sherry was not actually praying in the "correct" context of the binding principles because of missing some earlier teaching which brings me to my point. Sherry was praying with the understanding she had and, most importantly of all, she was praying in full faith that Matthew 16:19 meant exactly what it said: Whatsoever she would bind on earth, God would bind in heaven. Answers came every time she prayed.

Sherry is taking back her rightful possessions and the rights of others. She is receiving restoration and renewal by adding to her understanding one facet at a time. Oh, yes, Sherry now "does the loosing," too!

The Bottom Line

A full, theologically perfect understanding of this type of praying is not required before you will see God move to meet what you set in motion. You bind on earth, He'll bind in heaven. You loose on earth, He'll loose in heaven. That is the bottom line.

My initial efforts which were incorrectly aimed at loosing and destroying Satan's "bridges" still produced results. The targets were incorrect, but the principle set in motion was right on track! I didn't know it, but I was tearing up and tearing down strongholds I had erected in the mistaken belief that I was protecting myself. I had lived most of my life with a false sense of security from their walls and yet Satan was using them regularly to access and attack me.

I had been giving the enemy full credit for almost every negative hindrance in my life. As much as he would have liked for me to continue to believe that, it wasn't true. I was responsible for my reactions to my past and for the distorted concepts I insisted on clinging to. I had refused to relinquish them to allow room to receive the truth promised to me in the Word. As I became aware of this, I was forced to confront some ugly things in me that I couldn't blame on Satan any longer.

There were many strongholds I had built that had protected the wrong concepts and opinions I currently held about my life. When they starting coming down, I really didn't like acknowledging the things that were beginning to surface. Fear kicked in on several occasions and I pulled back, saying, "God, I'm sorry, but I'm really not ready for this." I was walking in totally uncharted territory and I became fearful more than once that I might be creating something that would overpower me.

There was no one I could call to receive assurance that I was "doing it right" and there were no books I could read to give me a better understanding of what I was going through. In fact, several of my quite spiritual friends were leery of what I was entering into and suggested I should stop. That was a big help to my insecurities! After many jerky stops and starts, I decided I just had to trust the Holy Spirit's faithfulness to show me if I was being deceived.

I had to trust my realization that God had appeared to keep this subject before me for years, almost as if He were waiting for me to test it. I had to keep on walking in it.

Binding yourself to the truth and loosing the protective strongholds around all deception to confront what is exposed is not pain-free. Yet, having bound myself to His will and purposes, I believed He had bound me to them in heaven. Therefore, everything was happening with His knowledge and for His good purposes, if my "theory" was right. This was when I determined just how far I wanted to go with this revelation and that was as far as He wanted me to go. Since I was walking in what I believed to be complete faith in His Word, I was trusting He'd jerk the rug out if I walked too far.

Dealing With Memories That Deceive

I have worked hard at being an achiever, an over-achiever really, most of my adult life. Yet in years past, memories of failures and a sense of inadequacy would frequently spring up in my face as I began to accomplish important goals. These memories had the power to make me feel I had somehow just managed to con everyone, including myself, into believing I could do anything right. I would become overwhelmed with the feeling that everything in my life was about to finally collapse around me like a flimsily constructed house of cards.

Since my prayers had never seemed to stop these feelings, I concluded my beliefs about the memories must be right. I did not understand that I had erected such high walls of protection about these lies that the Holy Spirit couldn't get any truth to them. Circumstances continued to come, triggering reinforcement of these wrong beliefs.

I reminded the Lord, again and again, that the Word said I was a new creature and old things were supposed to be passed away. I begged Him to take these bad memories and feelings away. But "holy amnesia" was not the solution. You cannot loose, dissolve or melt the unpleasant things in your past, but you can realign them with the truth and neutralize their ability to hurt you anymore. You can straighten out and render unhappy memories powerless over the reality of today.

As you bind and loose in prayer, bad memories will be stripped of the garbage and baggage they are so encumbered with. They will rise to the surface of your mind, covered by a stable and fixed (91:1) trust that God will make them okay. You will finally be able to stop justifying your right to both protect and to hold onto those memories, keeping them painfully infused with life.

No Holy Amnesia

Holy amnesia is not the answer. If you were able to destroy your past, how would you ever be able to tell of God's goodness to heal and restore? How would you be able to express how much He had done for you? Your memories are permanently imprinted in the cells of your brain. That's the way the brain works. While it is true memories can be blocked by trauma or severe denial, they can also suddenly resurface when triggered by certain circumstances. This is a tactic the enemy works very hard to set up. Remember this, you may have managed to temporarily block out certain memories, but Satan knows every painful thing that ever happened to you and is always ready to reactivate the pain when he gets a chance.

You can expose those memories to God's truth and healing and close the door on their power to hurt. In fact, you can slam the door right in Satan's screaming red face! Just always remember to bind yourself to the truth and the will of God and the mind of Christ before you start the loosing. The binding is where the stability and fixed trust come from—the binding gives you strength and allows no room for fear. God's perfect love casts out fear!

Then loose the power and effects of those memories and loose the strongholds guarding them. Loose wrong ideas and beliefs and any deception associated with what you remember. Repent and loose wrong patterns of thinking and beliefs you have had about whoever was associated with the memories. Surrender them and yourself completely to God's healing power.

Many Christians do not realize they are adamantly resisting any surrender of their bad memories. They replay their inner tapes of anger and guilt over bad memories, failures and humiliations like those old eight-track tapes that never stopped. The simplest attempts at binding and loosing will jerk their tape player's plug! The only step the hurting Christian needs to make is to choose to do it and trust God with the consequences which will bring restoration and renewal and freedom.

Remember, your past's only function is to be the part of your life you have learned from and overcome. It is your reference point to show the magnitude of what God has done for you so you can show others what He will do for them.

As I began to loose the negative things in my life, I took a crack at almost everything. I loosed the negative influences of the world from myself. I crushed and smashed the deceptions of the enemy trying to confuse me. I tore apart, wrecked, cracked, crushed and ripped asunder the effects of work of the enemy in every area of my life...in my finances, my family, my home and my work. Although I would refine my prayers and spiritual warfare through experience, I saw answers right away.

I began to see my own attitudes causing me to reject those who brought offenses. I began to see old patterns of thinking causing me to reject opportunities. I began to see I was addicted to certain patterns of negative thinking. And I went after them and loosed them! I also began to see wrong attitudes and patterns of thinking in everyone else, as well, becoming quite the "attitude inspector." Finding many of these attitudes had a near relative working in me, I knew why I had recognized them so quickly. I was amazed any of us had been getting anywhere at all!

The strongholds were beginning to be torn down and I was peeking tentatively over the top of the rubble, excited by what I saw. Yet I was still clinging to bits of the pieces of the only protection I felt I had ever had. The work of restoration continued in my life and for the first time, I was cooperating by using the spiritual keys and weapons Jesus has given me.

Our Spiritual Weapons

Second Corinthians 10:4-5 (KJV) tells us "...the weapons of our warfare are not carnal, but mighty through God to the pulling down of strong holds. Casting down imaginations, and every high thing that exalteth itself against the knowledge of God, and bringing into captivity every thought to the obedience of Christ."

Our weapons are not carnal; they are spiritual. This passage clearly tells us the weapons to tear down what is defeating us will not come from carnal, human avenues of help. We will never find the answers to our personal problems and true needs from the psychiatrists, the government, the judicial systems, educational systems, the military or anything else except God. We must take His weapons and begin to take down our strongholds ourselves.

Strongholds are established in different ways. Three of these ways are:

1) Personal strongholds in individual lives.
2) Ideologies and philosophies such as communism and humanism.
3) Cultural, geographical and political sources.

There are those who relate the tearing down of strongholds to spiritual warfare waged against principalities, powers, rulers of darkness of this world and spiritual wickedness in high places. They teach spiritual warfare is to be waged against these levels of satanic influence as they have been discerned in different areas and then warred with accordingly.

There is merit in these teachings, not the least of which is supported in part by the archangel Michael being sent to war together with the angel being withstood by the prince of the kingdom of Persia in the Book of Daniel. However, I wish to focus upon the effects of personal strongholds within the individual. No higher level or broader scope of strongholds will ever be effectively attacked and destroyed by those who remain imprisoned by their own inner strongholds.

The tearing down and destroying of the sources of personal strongholds can be categorized into two areas. The first area consists of seven sources of inner influence: attitudes, patterns of thinking, ideas, desires, beliefs, habits and behaviors learned from ungodly sources. The second area consists of two sources of outside influence: generational bondages and wrong words (word curses) spoken about us, to us and by us. (I will discuss the last two categories in a later chapter.)

Our old nature seems to have some sort of "spiritual" velcro that grabs and tightly holds onto every wrong thing issuing from the above sources and influences.

Crucifying the Old Nature

The Bible says we, and I repeat we, are to crucify our sinful old natures. Every believer has heard that many times. I used to wish desperately for guidelines, keys or anything to help me know exactly how to do what the following verses say: "...Walk and live habitually in the (Holy) Spirit—responsive to and controlled and guided by the Spirit...those who belong to Christ Jesus, the Messiah, have crucified the flesh—the Godless human nature—with its passions and appetites and desires. If we live by the (Holy) Spirit, let us also walk by the Spirit—if by the (Holy) Spirit we have our life (in God), let us go forward walking in line, our conduct controlled by the Spirit" (Gal. 5:16,24-25 TAB).

Christians accomplish this to some degree by giving up the obvious things, generally external actions and behaviors: drinking, smoking, cursing, gambling, drugs, fornication, to name a few of the most obvious things most new Christians first learn to crucify. Unfortunately, these accomplishments can be simply modifications of external behaviors attained through sheer human will power.

It is far more difficult to know how to go after the actual internal sources of the manifested behaviors. Those sources can only be found in the old nature hiding behind strongholds in the crevices and cracks of your inner being. That old nature, left to its devices, continues to generate wrong desires even though external behavior has seemingly been crucified. This is a source of real distress and heartache for many who long to be free from old ways, yet continue to fight them day after day.

The following inner influences are the sources the old nature has convinced us to accept and then build strongholds around. Discover how to expose and loose these sources and their strongholds and you have discovered the keys to crucifying your old nature and your flesh. Many of these influences and strongholds tend to overlap, making it difficult to categorize them exclusively as one or the other. Don't be concerned if they appear to overlap, just loose them and get rid of them!

Wrong Attitudes

I remember when saying someone had a real "attitude" was a very negative statement. Today, when someone or something has "a real attitude," it denotes desirability. Attitude is a hot word in media advertising in 1992. I have seen ads for a music group, a car, a beautiful woman and a famous television actor all touted as having "attitude," translated superiority, power, arrogance. Attitude is bankable in the decade of the nineties.

My 1946 Webster's Dictionary defines attitude as an instinctive mental reaction that reveals an opinion. My 1977 Webster's Dictionary defines attitude as a mental position or feeling toward something or a position assumed for a specific purpose. The media of the nineties "describes" attitude as superiority, charisma, importance and power.

We have spent our whole lives acquiring various attitudes, some good and some quite destructive to ourselves and others. The only right attitudes we should strive to convey as Christians are attitudes expressed by the fruit of the Spirit in Galatians 5:22-26 (NIV), "...Love, joy, peace, patience, kindness, goodness, faithfulness, gentleness and self-control...those who belong to Christ Jesus have crucified the sinful nature with its passions and desires. Since we live by the Spirit, let us keep in step with the Spirit. Let us not become conceited, provoking and envying each other."

We can begin to accomplish this by binding our minds to the mind of Christ and loosing all wrong attitudes and the strongholds around them. Some of the most obvious wrong attitudes include self-centeredness, unforgiveness, bitterness, negativity, meanness and impatience. Begin by loosing all wrong attitudes in general and the strongholds that protect them. In a relatively short while, specific attitudes will be revealed that you can loose by name. You may be quite shocked at some of the attitudes that have been hindering you.

Wrong Patterns of Thinking

The word "pattern" has many meanings, but one of its more unusual meanings best describes the "wrong patterns of thinking" the Lord spoke of to me. Pattern means, among other things, the model used to make a mold into which molten metal is poured to form a casting. This pattern/mold is so rigid, it can hold and shape molten metal. Regardless of what you pour in—liquid gold, molten metal, wet cement or gelatin—the end result will come out shaped exactly the same way every time.

The act of thinking is how we form our thoughts in our mind. When mind sets (patterns of thinking) are locked into place in our minds, thoughts will come out of that pattern (mind set/mold) rigidly formed the same way every time.

Most of us know someone who is so sensitive that he or she is offended by nearly everyone. This person has a mind set that whatever is being said to them must be a put-down. Some people have been badly mistreated and their pattern of thinking receives and molds all input from others as attacks and abuse. Strongholds protect these patterns of thinking, giving the devil access to twist and distort them even further. With increasing frequency these days, we find dangerous personalities having emerged from these exact situations—personalities that turn into serial killers, rapists, psychotics, etc.

Someone mauled by a dog can panic at the sight of one because there is only one pattern of thinking or mold a dog fits in their mind. Those who have been abused and misused by people in power over them invariably view authority with a thought pattern of distrust. Someone who believes he or she has been persecuted or exploited by 1) a certain race, 2) a certain culture, or 3) a certain level of society will develop a mind set of animosity towards that entity. One example of this, covering all three of these categories, is the animosity that fueled the riots and looting which erupted in Southern California after the Rodney King trial outcome in April of 1992.

Anyone who has repeatedly been told they are stupid, ugly, worthless or a failure will invariably develop patterns of wrong thinking. Those patterns have the power to mold all future input negatively into a reinforcement of that wrong belief, overriding the truth. Some other wrong patterns of thinking include self-hatred, the sense of personal worthlessness, self-deception, self-destructiveness, etc. Any pattern of thinking that cannot be verified with Christ-like thinking in the Word of God will always bring defeat.

It is very difficult for the Holy Spirit to renew and restore the mind filled with strongholds built around mind sets and old patterns of thinking. As stated before, a stronghold is anything you rely upon to defend your opinion and position, even if you are dead wrong. Some will immediately say, "But I'm not wrong. Terrible things did happen to me." Things do happen and have happened to everyone that are definitely not right, not fair and not good. Those are facts and you cannot loose facts. But the wrong patterns of thinking, wrong behaviors and the strongholds that come from such existing facts can be loosed.

The following is the typical pattern of the "layering" that will follow a cruel, unfair or otherwise traumatic happening in a life that has not been surrendered to the will and purposes of God:

Something traumatic happens in my life which is **a fact** —> which leads me to develop **a wrong pattern of thinking** —>which helps me justify **a wrong behavior**—> which causes me to erect **a stronghold** to protect my right to do so—> **which perpetuates my pain by keeping the trauma locked in and God locked out.**

You cannot loose the fact of the original trauma or abuse, but you can peel off the multiple layers that keep it from being exposed to God's healing and renewal. You begin with the stabilizing of your mind, will and emotions through binding. Then you reverse the process shown above by loosing the stronghold, loosing the wrong behavior and loosing the wrong pattern of thinking to expose the actual hurt beneath all those layers so that God can heal it.

It is important to always approach the binding and loosing as a linked action. There is no room for the mind of Christ to be at one with a mind cluttered with old layers of defenses. And it can be difficult to continue loosing the "layers" when the mind begins to search for protection as it becomes aware that its defenses are coming down. When you bind your mind to the mind of Christ, as every wrong thought and stronghold is loosed and room is made to receive, Christ's thoughts, feelings and purposes (1 Cor. 2:16 TAB) begin to flow into your mind to heal.

Wrong Ideas

Your ideas are the representation of your thoughts on a given subject. It is interesting that the English word "idea" is not used in the King James Bible; the closest words used are thoughts and imagination. In the verses that exhort us to pull down strongholds (2 Cor. 10:4-5), the Word of God speaks clearly of the need for casting down evil imaginations and every high thing that would exalt itself against the knowledge of God that we can bring every thought into captivity to the obedience of Christ. In these same verses in The Amplified Version, we read of the need for casting down arguments, theories, reasonings and proud and lofty things that set themselves up against the knowledge of God.

By loosing wrong ideas, we are shattering, smashing and dissolving evil imaginations; wrong theories, reasonings and thoughts; and proud, lofty and high pretensions that set themselves up to oppose our further knowledge of God. It is vital that we all strip these things out of our old natures to make room to understand God.

Wrong Desires

Desire is a word that evokes many images. Webster defines desire as a conscious impulse toward an object or experience that promises enjoyment or satisfaction when it is attained. In the original Greek text, the word desire is described as (1) setting the heart upon and longing for, or (2) to intensely crave possession of something or someone.

Desire can be a right longing for something good such as a deeper relationship with Jesus Christ. A right desire could be for fellowship or beautiful music. A right desire can be for a marriage, as long as God is allowed to bring the mate and the timing. A wrong desire can be covetousness, self-gratification or self-indulgence. Wrong desires generally come from an inner drive to satisfy an unmet need that has been in your life for a long time, even from childhood. You can't loose an unmet need, but you can loose the wrong desires that have come from it and the strongholds around them.

Socially unacceptable attempts to get deep inner needs met often bring rebuke and ridicule. How often have you heard it said in disgust that someone's behavior was just an attempt to get attention or sympathy? The acting out of a need is often perceived and verbally labeled as a weakness of character or a personal failing. The needy person begins to see their unmet needs as failures and weaknesses rather than needs the Lord desires to meet. This causes him or her to build strongholds around the needs, hoping to hide them from others.

The problem is, the need still exists and it continues to exert internal pressure which manifests itself in the external form of wrong desires. The unmet need exists, it is a fact, and you cannot loose a fact. But you can dissolve, melt and destroy all of the garbage that has been layered over that unmet need. You can loose the stronghold protecting those layers. You alone can make the choice to do this and expose your need to the only one who can ever fulfill and satisfy it—the Lord.

Wrong desires have the potential to escalate into forceful, destructive drives to achieve fulfillment. Wrong desires bring about the destruction of marriages and wrong desires bring about wrong marriages. Wrong desires are the root of much of the grief and sorrow in this world, including adultery, stealing and substance abuse to mention only a few.

Wrong Beliefs

A belief is the mental acceptance of something that appears to be deserving of confidence and trust. Christians' right beliefs fortify and strengthen their faith which is the substance of things hoped for, the evidence of things not seen. But even a Christian's mind, if it has not been stripped of strongholds, can place great confidence and trust in wrong beliefs, turning them into a distorted perception of "truth." Sustained faith in a wrong belief can cause the erecting of a stronghold which will effectively block the receiving of God's truth.

Loosing wrong beliefs does not mean they will automatically disappear, but they will no longer be able to hide from you or deceive you. They will be exposed and you will be able to see them for what they are and reject them. Then, as you loose them and their strongholds, they will have to go. When you reject wrong beliefs, you make room by enlarging your capacity to receive and know truth that will set you free.

Bind yourself to the truth first. Then loose any deceptions the enemy has brought to you, all wrong beliefs and any strongholds associated with them.

Wrong Behaviors and Habits

A behavior is anything an organism or being does involving action and response to stimulation. A habit is an acquired mode of behavior repeated so often it becomes involuntary, fixed and sometimes compulsive. The world has come up with some very interesting ways to deal with wrong behaviors and habits. As a behavior or a habit is a response to stimulation, this explains the questionable theory behind using painful stimulation (such as electric shock) to modify undesirable behaviors. A milder form of behavior modification is to place a rubber band around your wrist and then sharply snap it every time you think about indulging in a behavior you're trying to quit.

Negative motivation will never bring about good behavior. It will only modify the bad behavior. Behavior modification does nothing other than making the outward behavior manifestation disappear. The underlying reason for the behavior will still exist and the behavior will just manifest itself under a different guise. Those who work with behavior modification know this and accept a less destructive behavior as a trade off for the better. This is a temporary solution. The better solution is to uncover the source and cooperate with God in dealing with it. Binding and loosing makes this possible.

Stress, pain and guilt can each stimulate a response of wrong behavior such as substance abuse or over-indulging in food. Fear of being controlled can stimulate a response of manipulative control. Unmet needs can stimulate the response of compulsive behavior. Negative responses of anger, cruelty, sarcasm and mockery, in fact all negative thinking, can become a habitual form of behavior.

There are many more forms of wrong behaviors and habits, but the important point is you can loose these wrong behaviors and habits and strongholds and make room within yourself for the restoration work of the Holy Spirit. You can also loose the power of their effects upon you and upon others.

As you loose wrong behaviors and their strongholds, you may find some falling at once. Others may come down layer by layer, perhaps stone by stone. But they will come down! If stone by stone, then every stone is a victory. The taking down of the strongholds exposes the underlying causes for wrong patterns and behaviors. If you have submitted your body and your mind, will and emotions to the will and purposes of God, you will be able to receive His healing for the underlying causes.

As you loose wrong behaviors, bind yourself to desiring Christ-like behavior. Bind your reactions and responses to the will of God. He will work with you and His mercy and grace will be extended if you struggle with the outworking of loosing certain things. But know this: God's understanding and mercy will never excuse or cover over these sins and strongholds. They must be destroyed or they will help Satan destroy you.

Whatsoever—A Very Big Word

I usually seal my binding and loosing prayers with these words: "Father, you have said **whatsoever** I bind on earth shall be bound in heaven and I know it is done. You have said **whatsoever** I loose on earth shall be loosed in heaven and I know this is done." **Whatsoever** is a very big word and it covers an infinite scope of territory. It is amazing how Satan has caused Christians to limit their understanding of this word.

Now, a very important point that the Lord made early in this understanding. Only God is wise enough to know where His plan for my life will take me. That plan may not include fame or great wealth or a certain mate or a certain career, so I would be out of His will to bind myself to such. I only bind myself to the absolute, known things of God found within His Word—His will, the blood of Jesus, the mind of Christ, the truth of His Word, paths of righteousness, the work of the cross. I have also begun recently to bind myself to God's timing which has relieved a great deal of stress from my concern over schedules and time frames. Binding myself to all these things puts me on the front lines of His will and His purposes, but it leaves the details strictly to Him.

Sticking "religiously" to these guidelines, I do not get into conflict with His will or the plan He is unfolding for me. Trust me on this one until you get into this. I assure you I have found that His plans contain all the excitement and thrills I can handle anyway! I just bind and loose the "whatsoevers," whatever they turn out to be, and then I fasten my seat belt for the ride.

After several years of praying this way, I have had exciting opportunities open up after loosing wrong ideas and beliefs about my future. Many years ago I was told to forget about being in the ministry and being a writer and either get married again or get a "real job." This put some serious bondages on my possibility thinking! But, through the understanding and experiences of binding and loosing, I have given all my possibilities in God the green light.

I am now an ordained minister, an associate pastor in an inner-city church in a metropolitan area, a published author and a field editor for a Christian publishing house. Those are some fulfilled possibilities I never even dreamed about when I began my relationship with God. And they aren't the end, for something new and exciting is happening all the time.

I do remember that as I first began to experience this new kind of prayer, I literally felt catapulted towards my future. I felt so free of restrictions, it scared me. I began to line up with God's will and became open to receiving. Some say to me, "You seem to get answers for everything you pray about. How come?" Part of the reason is I have finally made room to receive. The other part is that since I began to get rid of all my old concepts of God, I really started expecting wonderful things from Him every day. I believe He wants to give answers, so I ask Him for all kinds of impossible things for myself and for others.

One man said to me, "I used to think God only responded to prayers in three ways: yes, no or not now. But I've decided that when He got to you, He added a fourth response which is, 'I can't believe she asked for that!'"

I don't really believe God did that, but I do wonder if He doesn't look down and say, *"She really believes I'll answer that prayer. I will."*

When I finally penetrated this understanding, I was very aware it could be rejected, particularly by those who have formed strong beliefs about binding and loosing. So I began to share very carefully with only a few. After a mixed reception, I became brave enough to publicly teach this understanding when I received several timely speaking invitations in 1989. Some rejected the teaching and some seemed to be reserving judgment. Others received it as a fuller truth of what they already understood, rejoicing over new revelation in their lives. Several excitedly reported back to me with confirmations of God having moved in seemingly impossible situations and in lives that had appeared to be spiritually deadlocked.

Over time, I have been privileged to follow people who are still moving in this understanding. When you are able to communicate with a certain amount of excitement, it is not that unusual to find enthusiastic people who show indications of having received. This is not the true test of new understanding. The true test is whether or not the hearer is still rejoicing, growing and moving in the truth several years later.

SUMMARY

1. Full understanding is not required before you will see God move to meet what you have set in motion. You bind, He binds. You loose, He looses. That is the bottom line.
2. Our weapons for victory will never come from carnal, human sources: the government, the judicial system, educational systems, the military or anything else. Only from God.
3. Many turn away from wrong external behavior by sheer will power. The real victory lies in learning to crucify the internal sources in the old nature.
4. Don't be concerned that wrong internal influences and their strongholds cannot always be confined to an exclusive category. Just loose them all, no matter what they're called, and get rid of them!
5. The fact is: things do happen that are not right, fair or good, and you cannot loose facts. But destructive thinking, behaviors and strongholds born of these facts can be loosed.
6. Wrong desires, behaviors, etc. come from unmet needs and you can't loose a need. But you can loose the garbage around the unmet need to let the Lord get to it.
7. God's understanding and mercy will never excuse or cover over your sins and their strongholds. They must be destroyed or they will help Satan destroy you.

CHAPTER 6

Forgiving and Repenting

The Church has been remiss in teaching the full truth of forgiveness from the scriptural viewpoint. There is a catch to divine forgiveness that is often never mentioned. The Christian's forgiveness is usually described as a "free" gift from God. This is true insofar as you cannot buy forgiveness. But the believer's forgiveness does come with a price, for it is not unconditional. The Word of God says much about forgiveness:

- "And forgive us our debts, as we forgive our debtors...For if ye forgive men their trespasses, your heavenly Father will also forgive you; but if ye forgive not men their trespasses, neither will your Father forgive your trespasses" (Matt. 6:12,14-15, KJV).

- "And when you stand praying, if you hold anything against anyone, forgive him, so that your Father in heaven may forgive you your sins" (Mark 11:25 NIV).

- "And be ye kind one to another, tenderhearted, forgiving one another, even as God for Christ's sake hath forgiven you" (Eph. 4:32 KJV).

- "Bear with each other and forgive whatever grievances you may have against one another. Forgive as the Lord forgave you" (Col. 3:13 NIV).

We will receive God's forgiveness in exactly the same manner that we offer forgiveness to others. If strongholds protecting old hurts are involved, forgiveness can be very difficult. Yet forgiving unconditionally brings an incredible reward which cannot be acquired any other way. This reward is total freedom from responding to, reacting to and replaying those old hurts that still seem so alive sometimes. Forgiveness sucks all the life right out of them.

Still, some believe having to forgive everyone for everything, unconditionally, all the time, is an impossible condition to meet for their own forgiveness. They erect strongholds to protect their right to believe that.

There are times when God asks us to do something very difficult, requiring real sacrifice. Have you ever questioned Him at these times to make sure He knows your limitations and remembers just exactly what has happened in your life? I have. He remembers perfectly and He doesn't need to be reminded. We need to stop assuming that God only needs to understand our viewpoint and then He will accept there are certain things we just can't do. When God asks you to do something you are convinced you cannot do, it is time to start binding and loosing.

I've been saved since 1973. I had very little trouble forgiving at first, probably because I denied that the hard things existed while I forgave as many easy things as I could think of. Then, after four years as a Christian, I went through one of the most heart-wrenching wounds I have ever suffered as an adult. I had physical pain throughout my body from the pain in my heart. Another person was directly involved in creating the hurt and I wavered between striking back or building a stronghold to hide behind. So the Lord sent a new Christian friend named Jan. I rebuffed her initial attempts to befriend me, but finally gave in because it seemed easier. Our ways are not God's ways and He will use whatever can best reach our hurt.

She invited me to her home where she played a record for me, an album I'm still searching for fifteen years later. Jan's stereo and album collection were stolen shortly after that and neither one of us have ever found the record again. This album had one song entitled "Let Pain Become an Open Door." My spirit grasped at that and I somehow released my pain and it did not become a memorial to my hurt, a stronghold of unforgiveness and a stumbling block to the rest of my life. I used my pain as an open door to walk into the arms of Jesus. While He held me, I began the process of learning how to forgive when it's really hard.

First Peter 2:23-24 (TAB) tells us, "When He was reviled and insulted, He did not revile or offer insult in return; when He was abused and suffered, He made no threats of vengeance; but He trusted Himself and everything to Him who judges fairly. He personally bore our sins in His own body to the tree as to an altar and offered Himself on it, that we might die (cease to exist) to sin and live to righteousness. By His wounds you have been healed."

Jesus entrusted everything to His Father who judges fairly and then made provision for us through His own wounds. If we refuse to revile, insult or threaten vengeance when we are wounded, we allow His wounds to heal us and others. We can walk in this attitude when we have loosed former attitudes and old patterns of thinking and learned to react as Christ would.

First Peter 3:9-11 (TAB), "Never return evil for evil or insult for insult—scolding, tongue lashing, berating; but on the contrary blessing—praying for their welfare, happiness and protection, and truly pitying and loving them. For know that to this you have been called, that you may yourselves inherit a blessing (from God)—obtain a blessing as heirs, bringing welfare and happiness and protection.

"For let him who wants to enjoy life and see good days (good whether apparent or not), keep his tongue free from evil, and his lips from guile (treachery, deceit). Let him turn away from wickedness and shun it; and let him do right. Let him search for peace—harmony, undisturbedness from fears, agitating passions and moral conflicts—and seek it eagerly. Do not merely desire peaceful relations (with God, with your fellowmen, and with yourself), but pursue, go after them!"

Times of trouble and pain and offenses and having to forgive are not fun and I don't like them, either. But, if you look for the silver lining, it is that these times do not have to be senseless and unproductive. Rather, we can "...glory in tribulations also: knowing that tribulation worketh patience; and patience, experience; and experience, hope" (Rom. 5:3-4 KJV). The Greek word for experience means acceptable, proven, tried, trusted, tested—in other words, character that has been proven. If your character is being proven by "going through it," then use the experience to grow and to give God glory.

There must be room in our lives to experience the stages of growth our faith will go through to become overcomers. Untried, untested, untempered faith is not overcoming faith, it is baby faith. Babies do not understand the purpose of their faith. Faith is not given so you can avoid the hard times, it is given to get you through the hard times. Every time you come out on the right end of a trial, full of faith and forgiveness, you become more like fine gold.

As you pray the prayers of binding and loosing, also pray the words of God like this:

"Father, your Word says that tribulation can bring about a good thing in me. God, you know how much I want out of this particular trial, but I bind myself to your will and purposes and timing. Until I get out, teach me patience and give me the spiritual experience I need to be an overcomer. If I can't have deliverance from this situation yet, then I'm going to loose everything in my old nature I can think of to make room for

the growth of the fruit of the Spirit. Help me to be patient, help me to be forgiving and let me become experienced in the ways of your Spirit. You have promised your hope will sustain me while this is being done."

Dealing With Anger

The Christian cannot afford to indulge self by getting angry and grumbling over an offense. God has allowed us to have a capacity for anger because it is an invaluable component of the passion that lies within us to do bold and mighty things. But He intended our anger to be a holy anger like Christ's that would be converted into spiritual energy to bring justice and deliverance to others. Anger is never an acceptable response to a personal affront. There is not one recorded instance in the Bible where Jesus was angry because someone had affected His self-desires or self-interest. He was only angry at those who wanted to hinder His Father's will and desecrate His Father's house.

Still, Jesus knew there would be times when we would be angry and He warned us about giving room to such anger. He said, "When angry, do not sin; do not ever let your wrath—your exasperation, your fury or indignation—last until the sun goes down. Leave no such room or foothold for the devil—give no opportunity to him" (Eph. 4:26-27 TAB). In other words, Jesus placed a time limit on how long we could take to work through our anger. No matter how we look at the above Scripture, we have less than twenty-four hours to resolve our anger at anyone or anything. If we do not, we become fair game for the enemy to use the opportunity we give him to establish a foothold in our lives.

God clearly expects us to get our anger settled and dealt with before the sun goes down. If you get mad about something in the late afternoon, you'd better get it straightened out quickly. If you get mad in the morning, you can take a little longer to deal with it. Just make sure you aren't still angry, prideful, indignant, hurt, upset or pouting when night falls. The sooner we loose those kind of "feelings," the better. Such feelings will ride roughshod over our spiritual understanding every time. When they do, we have to fight the devil as we drag ourselves back up the hill to take that territory again.

Better that you turn to the Scriptures the minute you feel indignant, your pride is offended or you think you've been wronged. Bind yourself to the things of God and then loose wrong attitudes, patterns of thinking and any strongholds associated with them.

Then pray this prayer, based on the words of Psalms 119:165 and Proverbs 16:18:

"Lord, your Word says if I love you and am full of your words, I will have great peace and nothing shall offend me. Well, we both know I'm pretty offended right now. Either I'm sadly lacking in your words or my pride is getting mixed up in this. Either way, I'm at fault here. Your Word says pride goes before destruction and a haughty spirit goes right before a fall. Father, I'm in enough trouble without destruction and a fall coming into my life. Forgive me for holding on to such feelings. Lord, I surrender this whole thing to you right now."

The Things God Hates

In case anyone is still not sure God won't let them nurse just a little wounded pride from an offense, read Proverbs 6:16 (KJV). It begins with this statement, "These six things doth the Lord hate: yea, seven are an abomination to him...." What is at the head of this list of seven things that are an abomination to God? Is it fornication, homosexuality, murder, adultery, blasphemy? No.

The list begins with pride. "These six things doth the Lord hate: yea, seven are an abomination to him: A proud look, a lying tongue, and hands that shed innocent blood. An heart that deviseth wicked imaginations, feet that be swift in running to mischief, a false witness that speaketh lies, and he that soweth discord among the brethren."

Whenever pride, anger, hurt feelings, bitterness or self-righteousness over "unfairness" gets a grip on you, first deal with yourself through the prayers of binding and loosing. Then take the offense to Jesus in words that line up with God's will and His instructions like this:

"In the name of Jesus Christ, I bind my will to your will, Father, and I bind my mind to the mind that is in Jesus Christ. I loose all of my wrong attitudes and their strongholds, especially those of pride and bitterness. I loose all of my wrong patterns of thinking about this, including wrong beliefs about what is fair and how my feelings have been hurt. Jesus, thank you for being my high priest in heaven. I hold tight to my faith in you. I know you understand my weaknesses because the Word tells me you were tempted in every way just as I am, yet you never sinned and I don't want to, either.

"So I repent right now of the sin of anger and pride and wrong thoughts. Please forgive me and wash me in your cleansing blood. Help me to see and do the right thing. I will let this go. I will come to the throne of grace with confidence and find mercy and grace to do so. Thank you, Jesus."

Who's Going to Pay?

One of the most deep-seated beliefs in the world today is someone has to pay for negative circumstances in life. How often we've heard, "Somebody's going to pay for this!" Yet the hollow satisfaction of making someone "pay" rarely erases real hurt or deep pain. In most cases, no repayment is capable of truly making things right.

Most Christians would say they certainly are not revengeful or desirous of making another "pay" for an offense or hurt. Yet it is easy to slip into a subtle form of revenge without realizing it. Who hasn't struggled with some of these thoughts or actions at one time or another? "If you offend me, I will forgive you, but the next time I see an opportunity to do something for you, I will be too busy. If I have a chance to either bless you or Joe, I will choose Joe. If I see you after church, I will see someone else I need to speak to instead. I won't speak out against you, but I will withhold kind words, praise, reassurance and any outward expression of love because I feel you've wronged me."

Revenge is the act of retaliating by inflicting pain, hurt or loss to someone you believe has inflicted pain, hurt or loss to you. We must not try to settle these scores for ourselves, for this is the responsibility of the Father.

"Recompense to no man evil for evil. Provide things honest in the sight of all men. If it be possible, as much as lieth in you, live peaceably with all men. Dearly beloved, avenge not yourselves, but rather give place unto wrath; for it is written, Vengeance is mine; I will repay, saith the Lord" (Rom. 12:17-19 KJV).

Our Struggle With Forgiveness

Webster's Dictionary defines <u>forgiving</u> as ceasing to feel resentment against an offender. What Webster left out is that forgiving is not just the cessation of feeling resentment and a turning over to a higher authority for justice. Forgiveness must be a conscious act of the will to deliberately pardon another individual, period. It doesn't matter whether your feelings have ceased or not and whether God intends to judge the offender or not.

Then what about peaceful "co-existence," a slipping into neutral with the other person and ignoring him or her? Some Christians become very good at this passive method of dealing with their unforgiveness. They have ignored some things and some people for so long, they can <u>almost</u> forget the original reason. It might be something a sibling did when you were younger or it may be something a parent or another relative did. Perhaps it is someone you have worked with. Maybe it is another Christian in your church or someone from a former church.

You may convince yourself that you have forgiven this person and simply don't feel the same fellowship. How can you tell if you have forgiven and the relationship has just taken another direction? If you have any flashbacks of memory, <u>however minor</u>, of what the other person did or said to you—you have not torn down the stronghold of unforgiveness you have built around this offense. True forgiveness has a way of reducing a bad memory to nothing more than a fact of your past with no power to produce flashbacks. Do you have any flashbacks of what you had for dinner on July 14th of 1990? Can you remember at all? If you can't, then you truly do not hold any unforgiveness towards the cook.

What if you really have tried to forgive, again and again? When is enough enough? Jesus said we need to forgive seventy times seven...that is at least four-hundred and ninety times just to meet the minimum requirements. If you willed yourself to forgive someone every day, four-hundred and ninety times would take almost sixteen and a half months. <u>Once a week</u> would take you nearly nine and a half years before you could take your case to Jesus as having obeyed.

Jesus knew there would be times when forgiveness might be so hard, it would take an act of will over and over to forgive. This is why it is so important to bind your will to the will of the Father and then call on Him for mercy and grace as you loose stone after stone from old strongholds of unforgiveness.

There are no loopholes such as having to forgive only when the other person admits what they have done and asks forgiveness. You are to forgive whether you have been asked to or not. Jesus said, "...If you forgive people their trespasses—that is, their reckless and wilful sins, leaving them, letting them go and giving up resentment—your heavenly Father will also forgive you. But if you do not forgive others their trespasses—their reckless and wilful sins, leaving them, letting them go and giving up resentment—neither will your Father forgive your trespasses" (Matt. 6:14-15 TAB).

When you refuse to forgive, you cut yourself off from forgiveness. Forgiving and being forgiven are so closely intertwined, they simply cannot be separated. Perhaps you can live without the forgiveness of other humans, but you cannot live without the forgiveness of God. And, know this, <u>God will not forgive</u> an unforgiving heart that refuses to change!

Your will is involved in the choice to forgive, but there is no question of your ability to forgive. If you have been forgiven, you are capable of forgiving. It is that simple. If you have a problem believing God really has forgiven you, then you quite likely have a problem forgiving others. Those who knew little forgiveness and grace while growing up will erect strongholds around their inevitable wounds. These strongholds can effectively block out any recognition or understanding of God's grace and forgiveness. If this is your situation, you will probably bitterly defend your right to not forgive.

In the parable of the two debts in Matthew 18:23-35, the debt the king forgave was enormous compared to a small debt owed by another to the man who had just been forgiven. Yet, that forgiven man went right out and demanded a poor servant instantly repay a tiny debt to him. The man had been forgiven of so much by the king, yet he refused to extend forgiveness for a servant's small debt to him.

Avoiding the Tormentors

This unforgiveness cost the man dearly. He lost the forgiveness of the king and was sentenced to jail to be turned over to the tormentors. The implications of this parable are very clear. As believers, we have been forgiven an enormous debt by the King. We can lose this forgiveness by unforgiveness on our part and be turned over to the will of the tormentors. The original Greek word and its associated words that mean "tormentor" translate as:

1. Inquisitor
2. Torturer
3. One who brings pain, toil, torment
4. One who harasses and distresses
5. One who tosses and vexes with grievous pains of body or mind

These tormentors are the evil spirits of Satan, himself. When a believer who has been forgiven of so much refuses to forgive another, this believer is turned over to the will of these tormentors. They have other names as well—depression, fear, anxiety, disease, mental illness, poverty and nervousness, to list but a few.

The stronghold of unforgiveness can block all mercy and grace from the unforgiving heart. Peace and family harmony can be blocked. Divine healing can be blocked from the body, soul and spirit. It is a fact that the medical profession has documented diseases that are caused from chemical poisons released into the body by unforgiveness, bitterness, anger, resentment, frustration, fear and anxiety.

Nothing Can Replace Forgiveness

You can repent of your sins until you are hoarse, confess your faith to all, pray without ceasing, give everything you have to the work of God, read the Bible every day and still block God's forgiveness by an unforgiving heart. No amount of repenting, confessing, praying or reading the Word will ever cover over, atone for or excuse unforgiveness! There is nothing you can do that can take the place of forgiveness:

Forgiveness is not tolerance.
Forgiveness is not pretending.
Forgiveness is not forgetting.
Forgiveness is not generosity of spirit.
Forgiveness is not turning the other cheek.
Forgiveness is not looking the other way.
Forgiveness is not making a joke of a wrong.
Forgiveness is not politeness or tactfulness.
Forgiveness is not diplomacy.
Forgiveness is not a passive non-response.

Forgiveness is something much deeper!

Forgiveness is a deliberate act of the will.
Forgiveness is a full pardon.
Forgiveness is a substitutional act.
Forgiveness is obedience to God's Word.
Forgiveness is an act of love.
Forgiveness is the key to freedom .

Hebrews 4:12 (KJV) says, "For the word of God is quick [*it is alive*], and powerful, and sharper than any two-edged sword, piercing even to the dividing asunder of soul and spirit [*you forgive from your spirit;you attempt to cover over unforgiveness through your soul*]....and of the joints and marrow, and is a discerner of the thoughts and intents of the heart [*not the thoughts and attitudes apparent to the eye of another human being—but the hidden thoughts and attitudes apparent to the eye of God*]."

We've all heard people say, "Don't give it another thought, it's been forgotten." Forgiveness is not forgetting a wrong. You "forget" the hurt only after you forgive. When you try to turn these two acts around, you only send your feelings about the wrong downstairs to your subconscious. There it drips bitterness into your inner being until it causes something really ugly to surface later in your body or your mental state.

Strongholds of bitterness and resentment are like toxic thorns and thistles that root down in your soul. Once established, they will suck the life out of your mental processes, your thought life, your will, your motivation and your determination to live. Roots of bitterness cause torment in your soul, setting up deadly strongholds which the enemy then accesses to torment you further.

Remember what the writer of Hebrews says in 6:7-8 (NIV), "Land that drinks in the rain often falling on it and that produces a crop useful to those for whom it is farmed receives the blessing of God. But land that produces thorns and thistles is worthless and is in danger of being cursed. In the end it will be burned." The same writer also tells the Hebrew Christians they are in danger of losing out with God because of sliding back into their former ways and cautions them to, "See to it that no one misses the grace of God and that no bitter root grows up to cause trouble and defile many" (Heb. 12:15 NIV).

The Cost of Forgiveness

Unqualified, genuine forgiveness is the only answer. On our own, it can be difficult to extend. When betrayal or a wound from a friend or loved one knocks us down, our old nature wants to rush to our rescue, defend us and place blame. Forgiveness denies our carnal nature any right to cry out for pity, comfort and reassurance of what we have suffered at the hands of another. Forgiveness denies our right to protect our hurt, to pet and stroke it and pack it around for all to see. Forgiveness denies our right to tell our pitiful story.

Forgiveness says we will pay the price for the other person's act. This is what Jesus did when He died on the cross to pay for the forgiveness of our sins. Can't you see what forgiveness meant to Jesus? There was no holding back on His part, no grudges, no silent condemnation, no cessation of love or giving. He paid the full price for our sins—not with words—but with His life.

Much of the world's "forgiveness" is only empty words. People are very casual about saying, "Sure, I forgive you," when they actually bear considerable ill will in their hearts. Often the one who asks forgiveness and the one who says he forgives both know neither is being truthful. But the verbal social games are played out nonetheless.

After hearing "I'm sorry" again and again from someone, I asked one day, "What does 'I'm sorry' mean to you? Does it mean you feel bad about what you've done and that you are going to try to never do it again?"

This person looked me straight in the eye and said, "No. It means I don't want you mad at me. If I say I'm sorry, then you won't be mad anymore." The words of being sorry have become cheap to the world today and like so many other cheap things, they often have a throw-away value to the people who use them.

Real forgiveness is not cheap. It carries a very high price tag. When you forgive, you release the one who is guilty and place yourself in their stead. The saying "someone has to pay" really is true. When you forgive, you are the one who has to pay. You are the one to bear the loss instead of the one who caused the wrong. Jesus gave His life to prevent the loss of our lives. He was so serious about forgiveness, He gave His all for us before we knew Him or loved Him or even cared.

A hard, cold fact that many Christians don't want to face is that unforgiveness in your heart can send you to hell no matter what else you are doing spiritually right. You must be forgiven to be a part of Christ's bride. Forgiveness is not just a matter of being able to be at peace or have a sweeter nature or being more spiritual. Forgiveness is a matter of eternal life or death.

You must and you can forgive! If old memories of a hurt return to attack you, loose wrong patterns of thinking, beliefs and ideas again—and then forgive again. Loose the power and the effects of word curses, created by your own words and others' words. Bind yourself to the blood and the mind of Christ for strength and an outpouring of mercy. Bind yourself to an attitude of cooperation with the Holy Spirit's work in you. Bind yourself to the truth of the Word that says God will work in you to help you. You will find the strength and desire to be able to wipe the slate clean.

God Will Take Care of the Details

Trust God to take care of whatever else needs to be taken care of—trust Him to work out His will and purposes in every situation. Jesus did. "When they hurled their insults at him, he did not retaliate; when he suffered, he made no threats. Instead, he entrusted himself to him who judges justly" (1 Pet. 2:23 NIV).

The world wants us to believe we must be recompensed for every wrong. This is a message our old nature loves and it will lay hold of any validation, affirmation and reinforcement of the injustice of any unrighted wrongs in our lives. Society has made a multibillion dollar business out this validation process. What if God demanded restitution for emotional anguish and mental suffering? What if Jesus demanded reimbursement for physical pain and stress? Could any of us find attorneys who could help us fight against those charges?

The debt we owed God was so enormous, it was beyond anyone's ability to pay it except God himself. So the almighty, omnipotent, omniscient, omnipresent God of eternity, in the incarnate Christ, substituted himself for us and paid off our debt by shedding His own blood on that cross. The most precious forgiveness to exist came at the highest price ever paid in the universe. And it came to you and me before we ever had the sense to ask for it or the standing to "deserve" it.

If you cannot extend forgiveness to others, then you are a prisoner of your own strongholds. You are bound by unforgiveness, pain and destructive patterns of thinking. You may have no idea how to destroy them, but the Word of God gives you the keys to that very victory.

The world says, "You're entitled to your hurts and anger and destructive behavior! Look at what happened to you. We understand, let us help you get even."

God says, "*You can't hold onto those things, child. I cannot allow these sins to be covered over, you must destroy them before they help Satan destroy you. Let me show you how to make room to receive my mercy and grace. Let me show you how to forgive. Submit your will to mine and I will give you a new will. Submit your mind to the washing of my Word and the mind of my Son and I will give you a new mind. I will give you peace and power and freedom.*" This is God's way.

But, alas, God's way does not require a program, a group, therapy, surgery, money or a miracle product—therefore, the world will never promote it. Society promotes that which brings gain to the old nature. Greed is always ready to feed on unmet needs.

There are millions who are trying to find some way to heal hurts and satisfy needs they can't even articulate. It was inevitable that we would become inundated with what journalists are now calling the "twelve-step disease." Most twelve-step groups and programs generally began with good purpose and goals, particularly the Christian groups. But through them, recovery has become a way of life to untold numbers, rather than a means to the end of being whole!

It doesn't take a group, it only takes two or three to work out the torments of unforgiveness in your life—God, you and the other person. Sometimes it is worked out between you and the one who has offended you. Sometimes it is worked out between you and God alone. But you must loose every stronghold that would stand in the way of receiving His work in your heart that you can forgive. "It is God who works in you to will and to act according to his good purpose" (Phil. 2:13 NIV).

Let's get down to some serious binding and loosing to set you free to do this.

SUMMARY

1. One of the most dangerous attitudes in the world today is that someone else must pay for every insult, offense, loss and hurt suffered.
2. The believer's forgiveness is not unconditional and it is not unqualified. We receive forgiveness in the same manner that we give it to others.
3. Anger is an invaluable component of the passion within us to do bold and mighty things for God and others. It is never to be turned against someone who has offended us.
4. Forgiveness is a deliberate act of the will to pardon another individual whether you feel like it or not. Forgiveness is never just a slipping into neutral with another person.
5. Bitterness and resentment are like toxic thorns and thistles in your soul, sapping your mental processes, thought life, will, motivation and determination to live.
6. If you cannot forgive, you are a prisoner of your own strongholds. You are bound by unforgiveness, pain and destructive patterns of thinking.
7. It doesn't take a group, it only takes two or three to work out the torments of unforgiveness in your life—God, you and the other person.

CHAPTER 7

Setting Yourself Free

Using Your Keys

There are many ways to use these keys to the kingdom in successful prayer. As nothing more than a ministry of helps, I have included what I call my "training wheel" prayers. These prayers come from many hours of prayer by myself and others. Consider them spiritual "training wheels" to be put away once your spirit's sense of balance and forward momentum takes over.

It is very important to apply these keys to yourself before using them to pray for others. After teaching one woman about these keys, she began to earnestly pray for her family members and things began to happen. But rather than pursuing the victory, she grew fearful about the right "terminology" of binding and loosing. She became hopelessly entangled in semantics and ceased praying altogether.

Finally confiding her dilemma to me, she confessed she was afraid of praying the wrong way and harming one of her loved ones. She obviously believed in the power of the binding and loosing, but something was undermining her understanding. After a pause, she confessed this lack of confidence eventually cropped up in whatever she appeared to be doing well. Sensing an old pattern of thinking from her past, I asked if she had been loosing such from herself. She said no. When I asked if she was praying any of these principles for herself, she said, "No, only for my family."

Knowing this woman well, I was aware she has never been comfortable in asking anyone to meet her own needs. I believe she was hoping by unselfishly interceding for everyone else, God would "take care" of her needs. This is a dangerous idea that can get you in a lot of trouble when you are battling for loved ones. When you choose to neglect praying for your spiritual needs and strength, you end up functioning in your own strength. Regardless of how self-sufficient you may be, your mental, emotional and physical strength is not enough to deflect the attacks of the enemy.

You must pray for yourself to be capable of helping anyone else! You must have your spiritual armor in place that you will not become wounded and unable to carry forth. You must be solidly convinced of the truth of your position in God's love, your spiritual rights in Christ and the gifts and power of the Holy Spirit. This assurance will increase every time you bind yourself to the will of God and the truth and loose the old things of your old nature and its strongholds.

Daily Preparations

To quickly review your spiritual armor as stated in Ephesians 6, you need your loins girded (bound about) with truth, the breastplate of righteousness (bound to your chest), your feet shod (tied around) with the preparation of the gospel of peace, the shield of faith (joined to one hand), the helmet of salvation (fastened over) on your head and the sword of the Spirit (held in the other hand). The words in parentheses are the various meanings for Greek words for bind.

I try to remember to reinforce my awareness of my spiritual armor every day. Why? Look at these verses (KJV) referring to daily acts:

- David states in Psalm 56:2 that his enemies tried daily to swallow him up.
- David vows in Psalm 61:8 that he would sing praises unto God's name forever, daily performing his vows.
- David praises God in Psalm 68:19, "Blessed be the Lord, who daily loadeth us with benefits, even the God of our salvation."
- David cried to God in Psalm 86:3, "Be merciful unto me, O Lord: for I cry unto thee daily."
- Jesus instructed the disciples to pray in Matthew 6:11, "Give us this day our daily bread."
- Jesus told His disciples in Luke 9:23, "...If any man will come after me, let him deny himself, and take up his cross daily, and follow me."
- In 1 Corinthians 15:31, Paul said, "I die daily."
- Hebrews 3:13 encourages all Christians, "But exhort

one another daily...lest any of you be hardened through the deceitfulness of sin."

Working Out Your Own Salvation

Although Jesus Christ purchased your salvation 2,000 years ago and it is a completed work, our Lord deals with us on a day-to-day basis. Our understanding of spiritual things is to be an ongoing, daily pattern of releasing, receiving and growing. Since the enemy is ambitiously concentrating on destroying you on a daily basis as well, this is another reason it is wise to reinforce your spiritual armor on a daily basis.

God gave the Israelites the divine provision of manna on a daily basis. They could not store up enough for several days at a time as it would become spoiled; they were required to receive their sustenance from Him daily. Athletes know they cannot eat and train all day Sunday and then coast for the next six days and still be prepared. Neither can the believer "bulk up" on Sunday and then coast all week long, expecting to overcome whatever block the enemy throws at them. Solomon says in Proverbs 24:10 that we will faint in adversity if our strength is small.

Now, here is something exciting! Even though the Lord knows our beginnings and our end, His Word says He daily loads us with blessings. He considers our well-being every day. We need to focus on thankfulness for these blessings every day which keeps us from focusing upon the negatives of the world and the stressful circumstances around us. Daily gratitude keeps you from playing the old "what's wrong with this picture?"

game. You play that by searching for, making lists of and then erecting memorials to all the negatives you can find. Don't get caught up in doing that! Anyone can do that. A true believer will rise up every day and give God praise and thanksgiving and then receive good things, new every day, from Him.

Salvation is an ongoing, daily process. If you or I had received a complete work of restoration the moment we confessed our faith, we could have gone straight home to be with Jesus. But we are still here "becoming" new creatures in Christ. I believe we can speed up the process by actively loosing the old to make room to receive the new.

Quick Trip to Calvary

Let's begin right at the top. Jesus' thoughts were always on His Father, ever directed towards things above as He experienced life here below. He prayed without ceasing, His mind being one with the Father's mind. The believer can experience that same oneness with the mind of Christ and God. The Apostle Paul said, "Let this mind be in you, which was also in Christ Jesus" (Phil. 2:5 KJV).

We need to crucify the old nature to receive our transformed, renewed mind because the natural mind of man is not able to receive the things of the Spirit of God. I believe loosing old, wrong attitudes, patterns of thinking, ideas and beliefs and the strongholds protecting them is the surest, fastest way to accomplish this crucifying and make room to receive the new. Then we can have the mind of Christ. We must choose this unity of thought and attitude with Christ, it is not forced upon the believer.

"Just have the mind of Christ." Now, that is what some would call a "good word," as are many other exhortations such as, "Just let go and let God...just lay yourself on the altar...just reach out and take it...just release it...just give it to God."

These words are all well meant by those who speak them. But I can remember desperately trying to do, become, receive or "whatever" to make them happen. I remember evangelists praying for me and saying, "It's yours, now just take it." I wanted to "just take it so bad," I could almost taste it. I just didn't know how.

It is one thing to believe an act on your part would be right and good. It can be quite another story to apply a practical "here's how to" and then do it. Binding and loosing is the practical "here's how" to do it for making room to receive from God.

Knowing the answers are in the Word, many a believer has read the Scriptures and cried out, "I know this should set me free. Why doesn't it? What's wrong with me?" The answers and the power to receive and have and change are in the Word. Grace and mercy and God's help are in the Word. Yet the answers seem to elude the reach of so many. Why?

The devil gets far too much credit for hindering believers. It is you and I who have built up strongholds in our lives that keep us from receiving from the mind of Christ, from the Word, from God's truth. We build them to protect what we have come to believe and lock out everything else. These strongholds can become so impenetrable that nothing gets in that won't fit our accepted patterns of receiving. The Word speaks of those who oppose themselves. This is exactly what we often do even when we don't want to.

Releasing Misconceptions

We all have some desire, often a great desire, to surrender to the wishes of the Lord. A heart that is wounded, full of fear and unmet needs will resist that surrendering. A heart that is restored and full of love will respond to God's every wish. Obedience to the will of God is a natural outflow of a heart and soul that has been cleansed of the misconceptions of the old nature. God has promised He will work in you to help you accomplish this, but you must stop clinging to those misconceptions out of the fear of what might replace them.

Ephesians 4:22-24 (TAB) beautifully expresses what happens when we tear our misconceptions out: "Strip yourselves of your former nature—put off and discard your old unrenewed self...and be constantly renewed in the spirit of your mind—having a fresh mental and spiritual attitude; and put on the new nature (the regenerate self) created in God's image, (Godlike) in truth, righteousness and holiness." Notice the order here? First strip yourselves of your former nature and then "put on" the new nature.

It is a powerful step of obedience to bind your mind to the mind of Christ. Doing this will place you in a position to receive the instant you start the stripping by loosing. Not all Christians are willing to enter into the state of being stripped naked of their old nature with everything they have ever known and relied upon gone.

Making this choice means surrendering patterns and attitudes you may have long held to be your right.

Making Room

To be fulfilled and become an overcomer, we must be able to receive from Him. Behold, He stands at our doors and knocks. Far too often, this is the scenario when He does: We crack open the door and say, "All right, come on in. I'm sorry I didn't let you inside sooner, but it's so crowded in here. I really didn't want you to see." Jesus may be able to squeeze inside, but there is absolutely no room for Him to bring in His answers and gifts and restoration.

If your inner house is filled with the things of the old nature and all its attendant strongholds, there is no room for Jesus to bring anything else inside. All of your answers and blessings and understanding have to stay outside until He can get you to make room for them. Unfulfilled, unanswered and unmet, you cry, "Why won't you answer me, Jesus? Why are you doing this to me?" How painful it must be for Him to hear you cry, over and over, with everything you need sitting just outside the door of your heart.

I heard someone once say that most believers are always willing to welcome Jesus into their home and treat Him as an honored guest, but they expect Him to act like one. Everyone knows a good guest does not throw out things, rearrange the contents and tear down walls. A guest has no right to do that.

Stop making Jesus the guest of honor in your life! Sign that deed to the whole thing over to Him and then listen to Him! He's saying, "*It's time to renovate. Let's strip these old walls and move out this clutter. I've got some gorgeous new things for you just outside!"* Do what He says and then let Him bring in whatsoever He will.

We tend to fill up our minds (already cluttered with misconceptions of every size and color) with daily schedules, social activities, desires, concerns, work, family and the media bombardment of rumors of war, economic collapse, unrest and violence. These are the factors our spirit, soul and body come in contact with every day. It is easy to get caught up in the frenzy of these factors and neglect spiritual things when you have a partially unsurrendered mind. There are thousands and thousands of Christians who are in that state and not one of them lives in overcoming victory!

How should you pray for yourself to strip away the old things of your old nature? I pray like this:

"In the name of Jesus Christ, I bind my body, soul and spirit to the will and purposes of God. I bind myself to the truth of God. I bind myself to an awareness of the power of the blood of Jesus working in my life every day. I bind my mind to the mind of Christ that I can have the thoughts, purposes and feelings of His heart in me. I bind my feet to the paths you have ordained for me to walk, God, that my steps will be strong and steady. I bind myself to the work of the cross with all of its mercy, truth, love, power, forgiveness and dying to self.

"In the name of Jesus Christ, I bind the strong man and I loose his hold on everything he has ever stolen from me. I rebuke his works and loose the power and effects of every deception, device and influence he wants to bring against me.

"Lord, I repent of having wrong attitudes and thoughts, I renounce them now and ask your forgiveness. I loose every

old, wrong pattern of thinking, attitude, idea, desire, belief, habit and behavior that may still be working in me. I tear down, crush, smash and destroy every stronghold I have erected to protect them. I bind myself to the attitudes and patterns of Jesus Christ. I bind myself to the overcoming behavior and spiritual desires that line up with the fruit of the Holy Spirit.

"Father, I loose any stronghold in my life protecting wrong feelings I have against anyone. Forgive me as I forgive those who have caused me pain, loss or grief. I loose any desire for retribution or redress. In the name of Jesus, I loose the power and the effects of any harsh or hard words (word curses) spoken about me, to me or by me. I loose any strongholds connected with them. I loose all generational bondages and their strongholds from myself. Thank you, Jesus, that you have promised whatsoever I bind and loose on earth will be bound and loosed in heaven. Amen."

Word Curses

Spoken words do contain power to affect us. If someone has spoken evil, harsh words to you or to others about you, these words contain power to hurt. Hard, unkind words you have spoken about others or directly to them have the power to hurt them and then backlash on you as well.

1. Job said in anguish to his "friends," "How long will you torment and crush me with words?" (Job 19:2 NIV).
2. David prayed in Psalms 64:2-3 (TAB), "Hide me from the secret counsel and conspiracy of the ungodly, from the scheming of evildoers who whet

their tongue like a sword, who aim venomous words like arrows."

3. In Psalm 109:3 (KJV) the Psalmist said, "They compassed me about also with words of hatred...."
4. Proverbs 18:8 (KJV), "The words of a talebearer are as wounds."
5. Matthew 12:37 (KJV), "...By thy words...thou shalt be condemned...."

God has said no weapon formed against you shall harm you if you are His child, but cruel and harsh words can bring pain and trouble. I have been under harsh attacks of words at times. I have precipitated some attacks through a careless attitude or wrong words on my part, and some attacks have simply been instigated by others. Binding my mind to the truth and the mind of Christ reminds me to identify the spiritual warfare and remember that the victory for this battle does <u>not</u> come by any dealings with flesh and blood.

In earlier days of this understanding, I found (and still generally do) that loosing wrong attitudes and patterns of thinking on my part, after harsh words had been spoken to me, would usually bring peace and strengthening. But there were times I felt strengthened after my usual loosing of the power and effects of such word curses, yet that peace just wouldn't settle. I learned that if I had dealt fully with my own attitudes, this lack of peace meant there was further work to be done in the spirit world. Through these times, the Lord taught me the necessity of loosing the power and effects of word curses spoken about me. It often entailed quite a battle, but the peace would come afterwards.

I had been praying with these keys of binding and loosing for quite some time when some really hard, unjust things were spoken about me. As these words drifted back to me, I was amazed at how calm I remained. In years past, I would have been frothing at the mouth to defend myself. This lack of "reaction" was one of the strongest confirmations I have had that the personal application of these keys to my old nature has worked mightily in me.

Old attitudes and patterns of thinking and reacting had been defused and destroyed. As the circumstances began to slowly unravel, I continued to bind myself to the will of God, to the truth and to the mind of Christ. I steadily received the Lord's peace and assurance that He was in control and truth would come forth.

I was also binding (the negative side of binding—imprisoning, chaining up) the strong man, Satan, and loosing his deceptions that were impacting the situation. It was this particular binding that brought me to an unusual awareness. I was restraining the powers of darkness in the situation, yet I couldn't seem to stop the flow of spiritual attacks that were hammering my mind and invading my dreams at night. There was something reactivating everything I was deactivating. It was then I believe the Lord revealed the understanding of the destructive potential of angry human spirits speaking harsh words into existence.

I had already been loosing the power and effects of word curses spoken to me or by me. Now I loosed the power and effects of wrong words (word curses) being spoken about me. I bound the wills of everyone involved, known or unknown, to the will of God. I bound them to the truth and I bound their minds to the mind of Christ. I loosed old, wrong attitudes, patterns of thinking, ideas, desires, beliefs, habits and behaviors from these individuals. Peace wrapped around me like a down-filled comforter.

There are many times when we need to bind the strong man and loose the effects of his influence from situations. We must also remember the destructive potential of unsurrendered old natures of others. When these old natures are filled with strongholds protecting unmet needs and unresolved pain, Satan can inflame wrong attitudes and relentlessly drive that person to lash out and inflict hurt. When these factors exist, word curses can be spoken into existence against you.

The Magnitude of Words Spoken

Consider what would happen if someone spread slanderous accusations about you. Even though most people know you well enough to realize the accusations must be false, a tiny seed of doubt can be tucked into their minds if they do not spot it and immediately reject it. The enemy will then work to feed those tiny seeds of doubt. Innocent actions and statements on your part begin to be examined for hidden meanings. Suspicion left to its own devices will always find something to satisfy its treasure hunt. Wrong words have the ability to impact how people perceive your life.

In the past, you may have been the victim of such wrong words. By the time you even knew about their existence, the groundwork had already been laid for hurt and doubt. Some people go through their whole lives living under the fallout of wrong words. I choose not to. I daily loose the power and effects of any wrong words spoken about me, to me and by me.

Right Words

We can speak words containing curses and spiritual death in them without realizing what we are doing. We need to practice the words of God, speaking in love, with patience and kindness in every sentence. We need to speak with humility, forsaking rudeness, self-seeking and anger. We need to loose wrong reactions to offenses, keeping no record of wrongs. We need to abhor evil, speaking words of rejoicing and truth. Our words should protect and express our trust in others, offering hope and showing willingness to persevere for what is right. These words will never fail us or others (1 Cor. 13).

When the words of God and the words of our own mouths link up, we have a special connection to God. Romans 10:8 says, "...The word is nigh thee, even in thy mouth, and in thy heart: that is, the word of faith...." Romans 10:10 says that it is with our heart that we believe, but it is with our mouth that we confess our way to His salvation. Our words have power.

"With the tongue we praise our Lord and Father, and with it we curse men, who have been made in God's likeness. Out of the same mouth come praise and cursing. My brothers, this should not be" (James 3:9-10 NIV).

Loose the power and effects of any word curses you have spoken upon others—whether unthinkingly or in anger. Repent of having spoken such evil words, remembering that to repent means to turn away from ever speaking such evil words again.

Some wrong words can be spoken into existence without harmful intent. If you have spoken negative words about your childrens' lives, those are words of spiritual death. Get on your knees alone and bind your children to the will of God and the truth and loose the power and effects of any wrong words you have spoken.

Then pray the words of God in Psalm 103:17:

"Lord, forgive my doubt. I repent of the words I have spoken. You are a good and faithful God and you will perform your Word. You have said that, from everlasting to everlasting, your love is with those who fear you and your righteousness is with their children's children. Lord, I believe that promise for my child."

Pray the words of God in Isaiah 49:24-25:

"Lord, my child is being held hostage by the enemy. You have said that captives can be taken back from the mighty one and prey can be rescued from the terrible enemy. You have said that you will contend with those who contend with me and that you will save my children. Jesus, I thank you for this. I thank you that the lesser power that is contending with me and my family will have to bow to your greater sovereign power within me. I bind the strong man that he will not be able to stop me from taking back everything he has stolen from my children. Thank you that my children will all be saved."

If you struggle constantly to make ends meet, bind yourself to the will and the truth of the Father and loose the power of any negative words you have spoken about your financial circumstances. Words like, "I'll never be able to pay all my bills. I'm not going to have any food. I never have enough money. I'll never get out of debt." After loosing wrong attitudes about money and the power and effects of your wrong words, pray the words of Second Corinthians 9:6-8:

"Jesus, forgive my words of doubt and negativity. I loose all of the wrong attitudes and patterns of thinking I have about money and bind myself to your truth. Renew my mind and attitude about your provision and my real needs. Your Word says if I sow sparingly, I will reap sparingly. Help me to see if I am holding back what I need to share. Let me become a channel of your abundance. You are able and willing to make all grace come toward me, not so I will indulge myself, but so I will have more than enough in all things so I can give and do and help every good work."

Generational Bondages

What are generational bondages? The Old Testament clearly says the iniquity of the fathers will be visited upon the children until the third and fourth generation of them who have not loved Him (Exodus 20:5). Iniquity translated from the Hebrew word *avon* means perversity, evil, fault, iniquity, mischief, punishment and sin.

Jeremiah refers to the fathers' eating of sour grapes, causing their children's teeth to be set on edge. In other words, bitterness can be passed to a second generation. If your ancestors had established patterns of unforgiveness, addiction, lying, violence, divorce or other sins, you can be influenced by these patterns even if you are a believer. Since we are under the new covenant, many do not believe this is possible since the Word says Jesus has broken the curse.

Far too many believers are not living in liberty and the abundant life. Their abundance is often sitting outside their inner being because there is no room inside. Because of strongholds, these believers are held down and held back by self-imposed limitations. The curse has indeed been broken and every believer can live in that freedom. But too many believers still live under the influence of wrong beliefs, ideas and patterns of thinking acquired from past experiences.

Generational bondages can be retained from past experiences with family attitudes and beliefs. These influences as well as any unresolved pain and bitterness from your past can keep you from living in the strength and blessings of your status as a new creature in Christ. Loosing generational bondages still impacting you can bring you into receiving the freedom Christ purchased for you when He broke the curse.

As I said at the beginning of this chapter, consider these prayers as spiritual "training wheels" until you feel your own sense of balance and focus in this manner of praying:

"Lord, I'm standing on the truth of your Word. You said you would give me the keys to the kingdom, that whatsoever I would bind on earth would be bound in heaven and whatsoever I would loose on earth would be loosed in heaven. Right now, in the name of Jesus Christ, I bind my will to the will of God, that I will be constantly aware of His will and purposes for my life. I bind myself to the truth of God that I will not be deceived by the many subtle deceptions of the world and the devil.

"I bind myself to the blood of Jesus, that I will never take it for granted. I want to be constantly aware of its miracle-working power to restore and heal and keep me safe. I bind myself to the mind of Christ that I will be aware of how Jesus would have me think in every situation I come into this day. I do not want to react out of my own human, carnal thoughts when situations arise suddenly, I want to think and act as Jesus would have me act. I bind my feet to paths of righteousness that my steps will be steady and true all day long. I bind myself to the work of the cross in my life so that I will continue to die daily to my own selfish desires and motivations and be more like Him.

"I bind the strong man so that I may spoil his household and take back every bit of joy, peace, blessing, freedom and every material and spiritual possession that he has stolen from me. I take them back right now! Satan, I loose your influence over every part of my body, soul and spirit. I loose, crush, smash and destroy every evil device you may try to bring into my sphere of influence during this day.

"I repent of every wrong desire, attitude and pattern of thinking I have had. Forgive me, Lord, for holding onto wrong ideas, desires, behaviors and habits. I renounce and reject these things. In the name of Jesus Christ, I loose (destroy, crush, break, smash, melt, etc.) every wrong attitude, pattern of thinking, belief, idea, desire, behavior and habit I have ever learned. I loose the strongholds around them that would keep me from being completely surrendered to the will of God for my life. I loose all doubt and confusion from myself.

"I have bound myself to the mind of Christ and I loose every wrong thought and evil imagination that will keep me from being in sweet unity with Him. I bind and loose these things

in the name of Jesus Christ, who has given me the keys to do so. Thank you, Lord, for the truth."

Once you have committed yourself by praying this way, the Holy Spirit will work with you to expose the root causes of the strongholds you have erected in your life. Roots can be very deep, but the Holy Spirit has no problem getting them out. Some strongholds seem to come down all at once, others come down stone by stone. As you are able to recognize and loose specific attitudes and their strongholds, they will come down faster. But, whether you identify specific patterns hindering you or just loose wrong patterns in general, the strongholds will come down!

You will find yourself very aware of the power of the blood working in your life. You will find the thoughts of Jesus ready and able to help you deal with the pain or hurt that influenced you to set up strongholds in the first place. You will be aware of God's will that you need to face certain things that must be crucified and destroyed. You will be aware of the need to loose unforgiveness and bitterness and anger and you will be able to forgive. Being bound to the will of God and to the blood of Jesus will give you the strength and power you need.

These are the first steps to becoming whole and effective and dangerous! Move in the prayers of binding loosing for yourself and then begin prayers of binding and loosing for others.

The next chapter is somewhat of a departure from what has come to this point. After prayer and the advice of my editor, I feel it is an important chapter that needs to be in the book. It is a story that tells of a major victory brought about by joining with someone else in prayers of binding and loosing to impact a third person's life.

SUMMARY

1. It is vital that you are binding and loosing in your own life before you take on the battle for others.
2. Loosing old, wrong attitudes, patterns of thinking, ideas and beliefs and the strongholds protecting them is the surest way to crucify the old nature.
3. Binding your mind to the mind of Christ places you in a position to receive the instant you start stripping the old nature.
4. Evil, harsh words spoken about you or to you contain power to hurt you.
5. Some go through their whole lives living under the fallout of wrong words. Choose not to by loosing the power and effects of wrong words spoken about, to or by you every day.
6. Loosing generational bondages makes room to receive the freedom Christ purchased when He broke the curse.
7. Whether you identify specific patterns hindering you or just loose wrong patterns and strongholds in general, they will come down!

CHAPTER 8

Sarah's Story

Matthew 18:18

Matthew records the words of binding and loosing in a slightly different context in chapter eighteen. "Verily I say unto you, Whatsoever ye shall bind on earth shall be bound in heaven; and whatsoever ye shall loose on earth shall be loosed in heaven. Again I say unto you, That if two of you shall agree on earth as touching any thing that they shall ask, it shall be done for them of my Father which is in heaven. For where two or three are gathered together in my name, there am I in the midst of them" (Matt. 18:18-20 KJV).

There are some who use this passage only in the context of church discipline and membership rights because of the preceding verses 15-17. However, verses 18-20 cannot be restricted to this sole interpretation. These three verses offer valuable keys to the believer who is exhorted to pray in unity with other believers.

Powerful answers come to prayers offered from hearts united in purpose and motive. When group prayer is combined with the keys of binding and loosing, the results are dynamic!

Lab Rats in the Prayer Laboratory

I have held weekly intercessory prayer meetings in my home since 1988. While most involved in the earlier groups did not readily accept the binding and loosing principles, I am convinced this weekly "soaking" in group prayer contributed to my receiving from God. In the summer of 1991, I found two prayer partners who would join together with me (like a three-fold cord) to consistently use these keys of prayer for others' lives and circumstances. Now attended by five members, these prayer meetings have been the prayer laboratory for the final "testing" of the prayer principles of binding and loosing. Much to their chagrin, I affectionately call these faithful prayer partners "lab rats."

Weekly we bind a number of people to God's will and His truth, loosing wrong attitudes, patterns of thinking and the strongholds that prevent them from receiving from Him. We have watched impossible situations begin to come into alignment with God's promises. Where the answers have not yet fully come, we know God has said if we do our part here, He'll do His part in heaven. His part includes working out all the details.

But one of the first miraculous responses to uniting with someone else in this principle of prayer came early in 1990. I am aware that the following story stands uneasily outside of the flow of the other chapters of this book. It is a grim confirmation of the incredibly destructive influence of addictive/compulsive behaviors brought on by unmet needs and abuse. But I believe Sarah's story is an important testimony for the power of the keys of binding and loosing when two or more agree in using them for another party.

Sarah's Troubled Past

Sarah, a young woman (thirty-five years old in 1990) with many problems throughout her life, was in tremendous spiritual and physical trouble at the end of 1989. Sarah had repeatedly been molested as a child and then was raped at the age of twenty-one. Unknown to those around her, Sarah became anorexic in her early teens. This progressed over the years into bulimia combined with multiple compulsive-obsessive behavior disorders.

Sarah had attended church and Christian day school and confessed to being a Christian, but she was deeply troubled in her spiritual walk. Small, childlike and never having wanted to grow up, Sarah found life as an adult completely overwhelming.

She began to rely on drugs in her teens, most of which came from several doctors' overlapping prescriptions for her many physical and emotional disorders. She also began using alcohol, dabbled in the occult and experimented with wrong relationships—periodically walking away from God. As her problems began to compound, Sarah became increasingly addicted to prescription medications. Dealing with multiple doctors kept a seemingly never-ending stream of pills flowing. Believing she would be an alcoholic as her absentee father was (a wrong pattern of thinking), she began to drink regularly.

Sarah frequently visited emergency rooms with severe muscle spasms (she was now suffering from fibrocitis), weight loss complications, dehydration and prescription drug overdoses. Each different doctor or emergency room would order tests, X-rays, a complete work-up and then more prescriptions would be written. Only once was Sarah was placed under observation for fear that the overdoses had been intentional.

The purging and bingeing of bulimia began to damage Sarah's esophagus, her teeth, her bones and her digestive system. Then the obsessive-compulsive behavior disorders began: cleaning countertops over and over, crawling on the carpet to pick off tiny pieces of fuzz, arranging and rearranging the silverware drawer.

Let Sarah tell you some of her own story:

Many years ago I couldn't stand the whispers I was sure I heard about my size. I wished, I prayed, and I played I was smaller and thus it began. I was introduced to pain pills at age thirteen when I was kicked by a horse. I discovered they made me lose my appetite and caused me to throw up. I learned to drink after that and found the same result held true and I lost even more weight.

At eighteen, I combined a handful of Valium, some vodka and gin and a kitchen knife in an attempt to take my life. I lost even more weight in the mental health clinic I was taken to, which pleased me. What didn't please me was the deepening depression I felt. Intense dieting, pills, alcohol and excessive exercising all took their toll, but I believed if I was only thinner, I'd be small enough for a father to want me.

I felt I was in a race against time. Every birthday that made me a year older meant I was further away from being some daddy's little girl. I had been to church most of my life, but I could not seem to realize God wanted to be my Father. Something prevented any truth of His love from comforting me.

My lifelong quest for a father figure resulted in my being molested several times, ultimately bringing a rape at twenty-one. After a divorce at age twenty-three, my weight rocketed up to 150 pounds. Panicked, I began to make myself throw up on a daily basis. This quickly zoomed out of control and no matter what I ate or where I ate, in others' homes or at restaurants, I'd have to rush to the bathroom to purge myself. I can't even describe the many horrid, filthy bathroom floors I've knelt on, clinging to toilets that were nightmarish. But I couldn't quit.

I began to have a growing problem with obsessive-compulsive behavior disorders. These behaviors are fueled by a drive to repeat rituals over and over, often into the wee hours of morning, before one can feel complete enough to risk sleeping. I even meticulously folded all of the dirty clothes in the hamper, driven to try to establish order in a world that had gone mad for me. I would become very angry with anyone who disrupted the neatness of my insanity.

I began to experience violent seizures which doctors said had no discernible origin. I was not epileptic. As I continued to purge, I suffered cracked ribs and a broken collarbone from the retching and vomiting. With all my doctors, only three times during these years did anyone ever suggest counseling. I went, but talked only about whatever abusive relationship I was in and then I quit going.

In 1987, I had two overdoses of prescription drugs. One nearly killed me, landing me in intensive care for three days and four nights. But still the doctors kept handing out the prescriptions and I kept taking them. Then my Grandma, who had helped raise me, died. In another two months, my father died from his alcoholism while he was lying in the back of a freezing cold camper just outside his mobile home the day after Christmas.

My world continued to crumble.

Prayers of Confusion

By the end of 1989, Sarah and her mother were becoming increasingly frightened by the circumstances overtaking them. Because of unmet needs and strongholds in her own life, Sarah's mother fiercely protected and enabled Sarah's behavior. Sarah, on the other hand, controlled her mother and others through her intense needs.

Sarah and her mother believed they were seeking God earnestly, but they were confused in their prayers and tormented by many confusing deceptions from Satan. Both were in complete denial of Sarah's drug and alcohol abuse and her anorexia and bulimia. When confronted by well-meaning family and friends, the answer always came that God would show the doctors what was wrong if it was His will for it to be revealed. Denial is a powerful stronghold that can immobilize people, paralyzing their ability to help themselves or others. Denial is a stronghold that has the power to kill.

Sarah reached a point in 1990 where her weight dropped to a frightening low for her 5'6" height. Her normal weight had generally ranged from 120 to 130. By early 1990, Sarah was a walking skeleton comprised of bones and a skull covered with darkened, leathery skin. It was at that time she began having severe organ dysfunction and skeletal pain.

Sarah's mother, family members, myself and others tried desperately to get medical help for her as it was painfully apparent only prayers and the mercy of God were keeping her alive. Due to red tape and the closing of several government programs, no hospital or eating disorder clinic would accept her as a Medi-Cal patient because they did not feel she was in a life-or-death situation. That was the criterion cited for admittance everywhere we turned—she had to be diagnosed as being in a life-or-death situation.

Time and again, intercessory prayer by members of the body of Christ would rally her back from the brink of death and her vital signs would steady and be amazingly strong. Ironically, it appeared to be her healthy blood and strong vital signs that kept her from getting help from the medical community. Sarah and her mother were still in denial of her anorexia and bulimia and the attendant esophagus scarring, ulcerated stomach and multiple symptoms were never talked about. Incredibly, the doctors who saw her did not seem to recognize them either.

Prayers of Power

Sarah's mother and I began praying together early in 1990 in a uniting of the understanding of Matthew 16:19 and 18:18. Daily, we bound Sarah to the will of God, the blood of Jesus, the mind of Christ, the work of the cross and the truth. Together we loosed the devices of the devil, the effects of works of evil in her life, wrong attitudes and patterns of thinking, wrong behaviors and habits and the strongholds protecting them. Together we loosed deception and a wrong desire to stop living.

Within weeks, Sarah ceased denying her anorexia and bulimia and her deep spiritual problems, confessing her need for help in these areas. We praised the Lord and rejoiced that the tide had seemed to turn. Shortly thereafter, to everyone's dismay, Sarah's weight plunged to a new low of eighty-four pounds. Little did anyone know how far it would ultimately drop. At that point she was admitted to a local hospital, suffering apparent lung, heart and liver damage.

As Sarah lay suffering in the hospital, she and her mother were simply pleading with God to just spare her life. I urged her mother to realize that we needed to keep praying the way we were, binding Sarah to the will of God at any cost, trusting in His grace and mercy. I knew we had to keep loosing the strongholds and the work of the enemy no matter how hard he was seemingly making it for Sarah and those of us who were praying.

And he was indeed making it difficult! During this intense time, my computer self-destructed and mangled a very important manuscript disk. Another prayer partner had a simulated heart attack during this period that the doctors still haven't figured out. Still another intercessor felt like she was having a nervous breakdown. There were some who wouldn't even pray with us. I can look back now and see what an incredible threat Satan felt from our intense pursuit of this new territory.

But we kept praying, using the keys in Matthew 16:19 and 18:18, trusting in the promise that whatsoever we would bind and loose on earth would be bound and loosed in heaven. It was during this intense period of warfare that Sarah broke through her stronghold of denial and confessed her anorexia and bulimia to her mother.

Strongholds Broken

A couple of weeks later, as I prayed early one morning, I clearly heard a word from God. He said that through our prayers, we had destroyed the strongholds the spirits had been able to access and these spirits would have to flee the minute the Word was spoken to them! The foundation for harassment was gone and the foundation for Sarah's deliverance had been laid. It appeared there was nothing left to do but to send the spirits packing. With great excitement, I contacted two of the strongest prayer warriors I knew and said, "The Lord says it's time. Can you go with me to Sarah's house tonight?"

One friend, a minister experienced in deliverance, came from out of town. Three of us then spent the evening praying and guiding Sarah through repenting, renouncing, rebuking and telling the tormenting spirits to go. Because of the intense binding and loosing already done, Sarah was completely open to this. She freely declared Jesus Christ, the living Son of the most high

God, to be her Lord and Master and then rebuked the spirits, telling them to leave. Several anguished spirits departed immediately. We all rejoiced and felt the tide had finally completely turned. But God's ways are not our ways.

A Desperate Trip to Arizona

Incredibly, Sarah continued to go downhill physically although she began to prosper spiritually, her spirit and mind getting stronger every day. Shortly thereafter, her mother's pastor came across the name of a Christian ranch/treatment center for anorexia and bulimia in Arizona. Contact was made and Sarah's hope began to mount, only to be dashed as the cost of this type of intensive treatment was learned. More prayer went forth. Another miracle occurred and family members were able to secure enough funds for her to go.

Using every ounce of courage she had and drawing upon the Lord for what she didn't have, Sarah flew to Arizona by herself. The trip bankrupted her minimal reserves of energy and she collapsed in the back of the car of the ranch owners who had come to meet her. Unknown to her at the time, this Christian couple kept anxiously watching her in the mirror, praying and questioning each other and God as to whether or not she was dying before their eyes. By now, Sarah's body was impacted severely with physical breakdown, including a yet unknown deadly disease sabotaging any weight gain.

Sarah loved the Christian atmosphere at the ranch, working harder to succeed than any other guest the staff had ever seen. She followed the schedules, ate the meals and attended everything she could. Yet her weight kept dropping. After three weeks of intense effort to stop any further loss of weight, it was obvious Sarah's body was shutting down. It was a devastating blow to Sarah when the ranch staff said she had to be hospitalized and it would have to be back in California. No hospital in Arizona would accept her Medi-Cal benefits.

Nothing Left But Prayer

Sarah fought desperately against this. It was only when the staff promised they would accept her back if her severe physical problems were brought under some kind of control, that she agreed to leave willingly. The staff and guests at the ranch were in tears as Sarah departed, believing they would never see her alive again.

Accompanied by a nurse, Sarah was immediately flown back to California for hospitalization. She was totally defeated and emotionally devastated and God reached down to encourage her in a very personal way as she was wheeled from the plane to where her mother was waiting. A woman seemed to appear out of nowhere and asked if she could touch Sarah. She took hold of Sarah's arm, saying, "You don't know me, but I love you. Don't give up. You're going to be healed because you have great works ahead of you." The woman then melted back into the crowd. Woman or angel, the message was from God!

After a week in a hospital, the doctors said they had done all they could and Sarah was discharged. It seemed there was nothing left to do except pray God would be merciful. These prayers continued for another four months at which time Sarah's weight had dropped to sixty-seven pounds. She fought desperately against this.

God's Perfect Timing

Unexpectedly, a local doctor decided to fight for Sarah and he began to lean on officials and administrators all over the state of California. Through this doctor's efforts and the will of God, Sarah was finally admitted to a major teaching hospital in California that sustained an eating disorder clinic. This was in direct conflict to all existing understanding, for specialized clinics in California were not accepting new Medi-Cal patients, except in life-and-death situations. Insane as it seemed, even at sixty-seven pounds, the doctors treating her simply would not diagnose her as being in a life-and-death crisis.

The doctors at the teaching hospital were amazed that Sarah had lost nearly fifty percent of her normal body weight, yet still had healthy blood and strong vital signs. She was examined carefully and doctors again shook their heads in amazement when they discovered she had no brain damage. Once the human body has depleted its store of fat and muscle, it normally begins to feed off its own organs, including the brain. Brain damage frequently occurs in cases of near starvation. God's timing had come and the doors opened right on schedule.

After four months, Sarah's eating disorders were stabilized as she underwent intense counseling and learned new disciplines and patterns of living, gaining thirty-eight pounds. Other physical problems which had contributed to her eating problems, including severe pancreatic diabetes (a disease capable of killing), were diagnosed and treatment was begun. Upon leaving the clinic, Sarah moved to Southern California to continue her recovery with another family member. There she gained fourteen more pounds.

Many concerned doctors and medical professionals had been trying unsuccessfully to treat Sarah for over fifteen years. None of them were able to find the key to the problems she was battling. After a few months of united prayer to bind Sarah to the will of God and the truth and the blood of Jesus, the strongholds came down and truth emerged. After a few months of united prayer to loose wrong attitudes and patterns of thinking and the works of the enemy from Sarah's body, soul and spirit, the strongholds were broken.

Time Frames

Sarah is now in a time of learning practical living skills and patterns of overcoming. Deliverance is often a process requiring a time frame we do not always understand while new, healthy habits and patterns are learned. For some reason known only to Him, the Lord has allowed Sarah's deliverance and restoration to be very slow. It is an almost imperceptible, at times, pattern of recovery over many months with perhaps many still to go. Early in 1991, she wrote the following:

Can I break through a lifetime of misconceptions I have taken from society and stored tightly in my mind? Can I break through and change? Can I step through the strongholds? My mind is convinced to persevere, taking a great risk to perceive myself as a grown woman after all. Perhaps maybe even a beautiful one at that.

Is it too bold to accept myself as anything more than a three-digit number? Do I dare put forth the effort to discriminate against a lifetime of misconceptions? Do I dare take hold of the challenge and lead it instead of being led like a dumb animal? Fear has been intertwined in my thoughts so long, it makes breaking through difficult. Difficult, but not impossible.

Sarah <u>will</u> someday share her story of the battle to stop defining her worth through the controlling power of a three-digit number—her weight. She will share with many who feel helpless and hopeless, crushed with despair over these terrible disorders gripping their lives. They will receive healing and life and hope from her story. They, too, will learn to see themselves as defined by God.

Reunion Time in Arizona

In August of 1991, a thin and struggling Sarah returned to Arizona to pay a surprise visit to a reunion held at the ranch/treatment center. Staff members who were still there from Sarah's first trip burst into tears at the sight of her. One discouraged staff member said that seeing Sarah gave her the strength and motivation to go on in her work at the ranch, for Sarah was proof that God still works miracles.

Sarah spoke to the other guests, enriching their lives with hope in God's faithfulness to heal. Even in Sarah's still-weakened state, she has an incredibly powerful factor in her testimony. She has experienced life-and-death truth personally.

Teaching From Experience

Early in my ministry, the Lord impressed upon me that I would never be a teacher of theory—I would only teach from experience. This has often caused me to cling to my faith in a loving God as I have realized new areas He was leading me to study and understand. After finally ceasing to doubt and ceasing to run from what God was trying to reveal, I determined to walk fully in my understanding of the truth of binding and loosing since early 1989. As I have taught from my understanding of my experiences with this truth, many have come and confirmed its power in their circumstances.

After teaching at a Teen Challenge home for women, one of the residents, crying freely, spoke out as I closed my message. She confessed that many at the home were in confusion regarding binding and loosing and had been praying for understanding. These women, trying to disentangle themselves from the effects and devastation of the deepest kinds of strongholds, received and embraced the teaching. I received several joyous letters stating how many had never felt such power in their prayers for their own futures, for the restoration of their families and for their loved ones who did not know Christ.

As I shared this understanding with a quite elderly Christian Jew in Southern California, he received the revelation with joy. With great excitement the following day, after sleeping on this understanding, he could hardly wait to talk with me. He reminded me of Israel's battles in the Old Testament where God would tell the Israelites to destroy the enemy's entire tribe and all their possessions—every man, woman, child and possession.

Destroying the Enemy's Works

Destroying the seemingly uninvolved women, children, animals and valuables following these battles seems excessive, cruel and wasteful to our contemporary understanding. But God was forcefully saying, in the strongest way possible, "*Allow nothing of the enemy to come into your camp, destroy every part and piece of the enemy's work. Destroy it whether or not it appears innocent or valuable. Destroy every bit!*" God is still saying that today.

Bind yourself to God's will and His truth and the blood and the mind of Jesus Christ—then go after the enemy and destroy every vestige of his work in your life and the lives of your loved ones. Don't allow one single, seemingly innocent or valuable thing that is not of God to creep, crawl or be brought into your camp! Loose every stronghold that exists, destroy every evil imagination and take every thought into captivity to Jesus Christ. Dissolve and melt wrong beliefs and wrong desires. Loose, smash, crush and shatter every deception and device of the enemy.

Every stronghold must be crushed, broken apart, shattered to fragments and cracked asunder by separation of its parts. Let nothing of the enemy remain—not one stick from a stronghold, not one wisp of an evil imagination, not one whispered word of a lie. Through the power of loosing, destroy even what seems to be harmless. You can do it by the words of your mouth here on earth. God will complete it in heaven and take care of the details!

"It is God that girdeth me with strength, and maketh my way perfect. He maketh my feet like hinds' feet, and setteth me upon my high places. He teacheth my hands to war, so that a bow of steel is broken by mine arms. Thou hast also given me the shield of thy salvation; and thy right hand hath holden me up, and thy gentleness hath made me great. Thou hast enlarged my steps under me, that my feet did not slip.

"I have pursued mine enemies, and overtaken them; neither did I turn again till they were consumed. I have wounded them that they were not able to rise; they are fallen under my feet. For thou hast girded me with strength unto the battle; thou has subdued under me those that rose up against me. Thou hast also given me the necks of mine enemies; that I might destroy them that hate me. They cried, but there was none to save them; even unto the Lord, but he answered them not. Then did I beat them small as the dust before the wind; I did cast them out as the dirt in the streets" (Ps. 18:32-42 KJV).

The difference between victory and defeat in our spiritual warfare is in finishing the work. We have had a tendency to tear at strongholds and rebuke demonic powers until they no longer seem to be a point of trouble in our lives. This is the "out-of-sight/out-of-mind" mentality. The enemy is more than willing to appear to have backed off if it causes us to believe the battle has been won. While we congratulate ourselves on our victory over Satan in this area, he's already preparing to assault us from another direction with a different weapon.

This same lack of going far enough has applied to our prayers for others. The next chapter tells how to get serious and get results in praying for the most stubborn cases.

SUMMARY

1. Matthew 18:18-20 offers keys to powerful answers when group prayer is united in purpose and motive.
2. United binding and loosing prayers can break through entrenched disorders of anorexia, bulimia, OCB disorders and addiction.
3. Denial is a stronghold that can immobilize people, paralyzing their ability to help themselves or others.
4. The stronghold of denial has the power to kill.
5. After fifteen years of denial and unsuccessful medical testing, binding and loosing prayers broke through the strongholds in a matter of weeks.
6. Deliverance is often a process requiring a time frame we do not understand while new habits and patterns are learned.
7. A consistent and persistent tenacity is crucial for victory in spiritual warfare.

CHAPTER 9

Setting the Captives Free (Whether They Want to be or Not!)

Binding and loosing prayers are very effective for unsaved, backslidden and rebellious loved ones. I also pray them for complete strangers, leaders, government figures and other nationalities.

The Word tells us to, "Keep yourselves in the love of God, looking for the mercy of our Lord Jesus Christ unto eternal life. And of some have compassion, making a difference; and others save with fear, pulling them out of the fire..." (Jude 21-23 KJV). Binding your will to the will of God and your mind to the mind of Christ helps you achieve the first part of this command. The harder part to understand is how to spiritually reach into the fire of Satan's kingdom to pull souls back.

There is a well-meant "logical" teaching that declares everyone's hands, perhaps even God's, are tied when souls don't want to be pulled out of the fire. I'm sure you've heard, "You can't help someone who doesn't want help." **I do not believe this**! Whether or not an individual wants help is not the issue. The issue to be confronted is what is causing them to not want help.

If an individual fell into shark-infested waters, that person would not refuse help and deliverance from certain death if they were in their right mind. Less dramatic, but who would refuse security, health, liberty, love, peace, joy and power? No one, believer or non-believer, would refuse such if they were in their right mind.

If they were in their right mind, no one would refuse help if they believed they could have it. Some might wonder who they would have to bump off or sell their soul to in order to get it. Unfortunately, there are untold thousands who have done just that in hopes of receiving such things from Satan. They sold their eternal souls to purchase a lie.

The real issue involved in pulling people out of the fire is understanding that they don't want help because they are not in their right mind. Those who are in confusion, guilt, unbelief, anger, depression, deception and/or any other form of torment are captives of their natural minds controlled by their old nature. These people are following an internal, destructive script that God did not write.

The right mind:

- Receives the Word and its promises with all readiness (Acts 17:11 KJV).
- Is capable of serving the law of God (Rom. 7:25 KJV).

- Is a renewed mind capable of transforming a person (Rom. 12:2).
- Is a willing mind (2 Cor. 8:12,19 KJV).
- Is a sound mind (2 Tim. 1:7 KJV).
- Has a renewed attitude (Eph. 4:23 NIV).
- Is the same mind which is in Christ Jesus (1 Cor. 2:16; Phil. 2:5 KJV).

The "right" mind is in unity with the mind of Christ. Any believer can partake of that unity, it is just a matter of desiring to do so. Remember the partaking described in chapter four? "Whereby are given unto us exceeding great and precious promises; that by these ye might be partakers of the divine nature, having escaped the corruption that is in the world through lust" (2 Pet. 1:4 KJV). The Greek words translated as partake/partaker mean participant, associate, companion, fellowship.

Not all Christians are willing to get this close to the thoughts and feelings in Jesus' mind. To surrender one's thoughts to Christ's thoughts means giving up wrong patterns of thinking and attitudes no matter how firmly entrenched or deserved they may seem. There are many who have professed their faith who have never yet surrendered to oneness with the mind of Christ.

I've already listed what you can do to strip your old nature to come into that unity. Now, what can you do for someone else who has never been willing to surrender to the desires, attitudes and patterns of thinking in Christ's mind? You can logically present the futility of their wrong mind set to them, backing it up with chapter and verse to show them their error. You can do this with some stubborn souls until pigs learn to fly or you learn to fly, whichever comes first.

The alternative is to stand on the promise of Matthew 16:19, "Whatsoever you bind on earth will be bound in heaven...," and bind their minds to the mind of Christ. God will bind their minds to Christ's mind in heaven and their thought life will then be in for a real change! Regardless of their stubbornness, they will eventually wear themselves out as they struggle to rebel and break away from hearing the thoughts Jesus would have them to hear. They will hear His voice.

Whosoever

God is so ready to answer your prayers for your unsaved loved ones. The Word tells us He "...so loved the world, that he gave his only begotten Son, that whosoever believeth in him should not perish, but have everlasting life. For God sent not his Son into the world to condemn the world; but that the world through him might be saved" (John 3:16-17 KJV).

The Word also tells us that God is "...longsuffering to us-ward, not willing that any should perish, but that all should come to repentance" (2 Pet. 3:9 KJV). Paul exhorts believers that prayer be made for all men, "For this is good and acceptable in the sight of God our Saviour; Who will have all men to be saved, and to come unto the knowledge of the truth" (1 Tim. 2:3-4 KJV).

It is clearly the will of God that "whosoever" should be saved and come into the knowledge of truth. Since Satan's goal is to control the will of "whosoever," you can best thwart his efforts by binding "whosoever's" will to the will of God. Satan will try to break that bond by hammering on the old nature. But if God sealed the bond in heaven, don't worry.

Remember the word picture of the baby bound to the parent by the baby wrap? The baby is sometimes kicking up quite a fuss about the whole situation—crying and screaming and squirming and twisting. However, it is still carried along according to the will of the parent, no matter how red-faced, miserable or fussy it gets.

It is not difficult to reach those who are broken and crying for help. The harder cases are the ones who are apathetic, in denial, self-sufficient or full of rebellion. They have so many reasons for rejecting help: too proud, rejected before, don't believe it exists, won't work for them, and so on. These poor souls have been deceived and have all understanding blocked from their blinded minds. "...The god of this world hath blinded the minds of them which believe not, lest the light of the glorious gospel of Christ, who is the image of God, should shine unto them" (2 Cor. 4:4 KJV).

Those who are under this blindness do not recognize truth any longer or never knew it in the first place. They are not in a right mind. They cannot see, believe or understand God's help. How do you help someone who rejects the only true source of help? Don't condemn them for not understanding or believing. They don't believe they are rejecting truth; they believe they are rejecting falseness.

Bind them to the truth and loose wrong patterns of thinking and beliefs from them so they can receive the truth. Bind a backslider to the truth of God and the understanding they once embraced and crush and destroy the distortions the god of this world has taught them. Pull them out of the fire and wrap them in truth by fighting for them behind their back in the spirit world.

Spiritual Battle

Persevere in the natural only if it makes you feel better. It probably won't make them feel anything but more stubborn. Even the most loving and sweetest of nibbling, nattering and nagging rarely wears down an unbeliever or a backslider. It only wears down the sweetly nibbling, nattering nagger. Why? Because it is very difficult to stay out of the battle of reasoning and arguing with flesh and blood when you try to deal with stubbornness in the natural realm.

Your reasonings, arguments and battles are not with the loved ones you long to reach. Your battle is in the spiritual realm, loosing the wrong things from your loved one's old nature and destroying the strongholds they have built to protect those things. Bind your loved one to the blood of Jesus, that the healing atonement of the blood will be constantly before and about them. Bind them to the grace and love and mercy and power and authority and forgiveness and dying-to-self work of the cross. Bind their feet to paths of righteousness to steady their steps.

In the name of Jesus, loose (crush, smash, shatter, disrupt, dissolve and destroy) the lies and deceptions the enemy has told them. Rip apart, melt and tear down the wrong attitudes and patterns of thinking and their strongholds. Loose, shatter into minute fragments and lacerate the evil imaginations the enemy has set up in their minds.

Bind the strong man and spiritually plunder his storehouse for them. Take back what he has taken from your loved one—every good thing they once held dear or had not yet recognized as theirs.

Do not be confused by the positive and negative sides of binding. Fire can be used to warm cold hands and cook food or it can be used to destroy entire cities. Dynamite can be used to rescue trapped miners in cave-ins or it can be used to blow up airports filled with travelers. Anything filled with power can be used positively or negatively. It's all in knowing how to use the power.

As I pray for others, I have a basic outline for binding and loosing prayers. To hold them steady, I bind (the positive, helpful side of binding) the individual to the will of God, the truth, the blood of Jesus, the mind of Christ and the work of the cross. I bind the strong man, Satan, (the negative, restraining side of binding) and then loose, crush, destroy, shatter, melt and tear apart all hindrances, devices and influences he is trying to bring against the individual.

The next step is to tear down the strongholds in the lives of the captives. This is vital to keep them from cooperating with the enemy's attempts to recapture them. You can pull them out of the fire, but you have to continue loosing their strongholds to keep them from voluntarily returning there. Continue loosing until the Holy Spirit reveals they have begun to take over the reins of their own deliverance.

This is a very important point to realize. You can only accomplish a complete stripping and tearing down of strongholds in your own old nature. You can definitely and powerfully impact someone else's old nature, but you cannot completely crucify that old nature. You can bind them to the things of God, stabilizing and steadying them while their minds focus on what they're hearing from the mind of Christ. With prayers of loosing, you can undermine the strongholds in their old nature and you can undercut the enemy's deceptions. You can give those you pray for every advantage and assist possible that they will be able to pick up their deliverance and take it through to full victory.

Loosing the Grave Clothes

Through your prayers of binding and loosing, you are rolling away the stones and tearing off the grave clothes. What are the grave clothes? Wrong attitudes, wrong patterns of thinking, wrong ideas and beliefs, wrong desires, wrong behaviors and habits and the power and effects of word curses and generational bondages. Once you loose these, then the final steps belong to those you have prayed for.

Jesus did not call out to Lazarus to roll away his own stone. Jesus told the people to do it. When the stone was gone and Lazarus heard Jesus' voice call him, he stepped out of his tomb. But he was still bound in grave clothes. Jesus did not tell Lazarus to remove or loose the grave clothes from himself. Poor Lazarus had been through quite a bit at that point and he needed help from his stronger brothers and sisters. Jesus told the people around Lazarus to loose the grave clothes and set him free. After the people obeyed this command, they stepped back and Lazarus walked fully forth into life. He had make the final choice, and the people had cleared his path so he could!

Training Wheels Prayer

There is nothing that stands between your loved ones and God that cannot be loosed from the following categories:

Internal Sources of Influence:
1) Wrong attitudes
2) Wrong patterns of thinking
3) Wrong beliefs
4) Wrong ideas
5) Wrong desires
6) Wrong behaviors
7) Wrong habits

External Sources of Influence:
8) Word curses
9) Generational bondages

Every one of these sources of negative influence is eagerly nurtured and reinforced by the enemy's devices. I've put this all together into the following "training wheels" prayer. Pray this prayer and you can totally disrupt Satan's entire program in someone else's life:

"In the name of Jesus Christ, I bind __________'s body, soul and spirit to the will and purposes of God for his/her life.

I bind __________'s mind, will and emotions to the will of God. I bind him/her to the truth and to the blood of Jesus. I bind his/her mind to the mind of Christ, that the very thoughts, feelings and purposes of His heart would be within his/her thoughts.

"I bind __________'s feet to the paths of righteousness that his/her steps would be steady and sure. I bind him/her to the work of the cross with all of its mercy, grace, love, forgiveness and dying to self.

"I loose every old, wrong, ungodly pattern of thinking, attitude, idea, desire, belief, motivation, habit and behavior from him/her. I tear down, crush, smash and destroy every stronghold associated with these things. I loose any stronghold in his/her life that has been justifying and protecting hard feelings against anyone. I loose the strongholds of unforgiveness, fear and distrust from him/her.

"I loose the power and effects of deceptions and lies from him/her. I loose the confusion and blindness of the god of this world from __________'s mind that has kept him/her from seeing the light of the gospel of Jesus Christ. I call forth every precious word of Scripture that has ever entered into his/her mind and heart that it would rise up in power within him/her.

"In the name of Jesus, I loose the power and effects of any harsh or hard words (word curses) spoken to, about or by __________. I loose all generational bondages and associated strongholds from __________. I loose all effects and bondages from him/her that may have been caused by mistakes I have made. Father, in the name of Jesus, I crush, smash and destroy generational bondages of any kind from mistakes made at any point between generations. I destroy them right here, right now. They will not bind and curse any more members of this family.

"I bind the strong man, Satan, that I may spoil his house, taking back every material and spiritual possession he has wrongfully taken from __________. I loose the enemy's influence over every part of his/her body, soul and spirit. I loose, crush, smash and destroy every evil device he may try to bring into his/her sphere of influence during this day.

"I bind and loose these things in Jesus' name. He has given me the keys and the authority to do so. Thank you, Lord, for the truth. Amen"

Reversing Parental Mistakes

One very exciting and powerful aspect of binding and loosing is the impact it can have in dissolving the effects of mistakes you may have made as a parent. And what parent has not made some big ones? I know so many who have become Christians after they have raised their children without godly counsel and understanding. Some become Christians halfway through the parenting process and make awful mistakes as they try to shift gears from reverse into overdrive without letting the Holy Spirit work the clutch. I really stripped some gears in raising my own children, both before and during my Christian experience.

What parent hasn't been heartbroken to see sons and daughters paying the price of their own mistakes? What grandparent has not been grieved to see their children repeating like mistakes while raising their own little ones? Is this not the sins of the parents being visited upon generation after generation? You cannot go back and erase these mistakes any more than you can erase the mistakes made by the adults in your childhood. But just as you can dissolve the negative effects from mistakes made in your early life, you can do the same thing with the effects of the mistakes impacting your children's and grandchildren's lives today.

Begin by acknowledging the mistakes you made, no matter how terrible or gross they were. Don't try to excuse yourself to God, just renounce the mistakes, repent and receive His forgiveness for them. The Lord knows all about them and He's willing to forgive you and forget them. He's more concerned with your cooperation in straightening out their tangled effects upon the lives involved today. Then you're ready to go to work.

First, bind your children to the will and purposes of God for their lives. Bind them to the truth and the blood and the mind of Christ. Bind their hearts to a desire to know Christ and the things of God. Bind their feet to paths of righteousness and bind them to the full work of the cross in their lives.

Then bind the strong man and loose every evil device he has brought against your children. Loose wrong attitudes, patterns of thinking, behaviors and habits from your children. Loose generational bondages (the passing of wrong behaviors and thought patterns from you—> to them—> to their children—> and on down the line) and loose the power and effects of word curses upon their lives. Do this daily.

As the Holy Spirit begins to work with you, begin to loose specific attitudes in your children as He reveals them—wrong attitudes towards money, towards God, towards other family members. As the Holy Spirit reveals, loose specific patterns of wrong thinking and attendant strongholds such as unforgiveness, bitterness, materialism, anger, suspicion, etc. Loose wrong desires and motivations from them.

A special note here: As you have practiced the principles of binding and loosing in your own life, the Holy Spirit generally will have revealed specific things to you. These may be specific attitudes and thinking you also need to loose from your children. They are easily passed from one generation to another because of the everyday exposure family members have to one another. I am not speaking of transference of spirits here, although I certainly believe it happens. I am speaking of a basic passing on of lousy attitudes, critical patterns of thinking, bad habits, etc., from the constant togetherness of daily family life.

Be careful to not focus upon the things in your children's lives that irritate you the most. This can cause you to loose symptoms rather than root causes. For example, sarcastic remarks are symptoms of wrong attitudes. Constant pleas for attention may be symptoms of wrong ideas or wrong beliefs (monsters under the bed, threats from a bully, etc.). Don't waste time loosing sarcasm and attempts at attention grabbing. By loosing wrong attitudes and wrong beliefs, etc. (see rest of list), you'll be working on the root causes until the Holy Spirit gives you more specifics. Concentrating on symptoms is like trying to fix a runny nose when the patient has double pneumonia.

If mistakes have already begun impacting grand-children or other little loved ones, begin at once to loose generational bondages and the power of wrong words spoken about them and to them. Begin at once to loose any wrong patterns of thinking or behaviors beginning to form in their young lives. Bind them to God's will and purposes and plans for their lives. Bind their bodies, souls and spirits to the blood of Jesus and their minds to the mind of Christ. Bind their feet to paths of righteousness—all in the name of Jesus Christ.

A Grandmother's Victory

As you faithfully pray, you will see changes come. I recently heard a woman tell this story. She had been raised by overly-reactive parents and had raised her children the same way. She was grieved to see her own adult child harshly reprimand her young grandchild. When she tried to speak to her child, she was rebuffed with anger and accusations of interfering. Upon learning the keys of binding and loosing, she began to apply them to her child's household. She particularly concentrated on loosing word curses and generational bondages.

As so often happens, she was totally shocked to see the results of her prayers a few months later. Sitting with her loved ones one evening, she was grieved to see the grandchild begin to act up. Wincing inside, she wanted to grab the grandchild and shield the harsh words that seemed inevitable. To her amazement, her grown child spoke calmly to correct the little one who smiled and said, "Okay, sorry." The evening progressed smoothly without another problem. Her prayers had been answered and old bondages and strongholds had been broken and torn down.

It works, I promise. You will see answers to your prayers manifested in attitudes, relationships and freedom within your family. You will see a new peace and a new harmony in their lives and in yours.

Stabilizing Your Loved Ones

As you destroy and loose the things of the enemy from your loved ones—whether they are unsaved, backslidden, rebellious or just apathetic—they will become aware of the truth and the blood and the will of God to which you have bound them. Too often people pray, counsel and work to bring a person to a point of deliverance and understanding and then leave them like the house swept clean, empty of anything to stabilize them when the enemy comes back. Because of their shakiness and inexperience with spiritual victory, left to their own devices these poor souls often slip helplessly under Satan's dominion again.

It is extremely important to bind those who have been set free to the things of God for stability and safety while they grow spiritually and gain strength in their freedom. How long should you do this? As mentioned previously, until the Lord tells you it is all right to stop.

Battle Behind Their Backs

I have prayed for years for backsliders who have known the Lord and then walked back into the world, blinded by the lies of the enemy. I prayed and I trusted and I believed and I waited. All prayers have a cumulative impact, for our prayers which are according to the will of God are never without effect. But I felt there had to be some way to tap into the Word and use its power to affect the individual more directly.

The Word says we are to do things like Jesus did, even greater. Jesus didn't say He was only sent to pray and intercede, <u>He said He was sent to set the captives free.</u> All of us know captives—they include children, parents, friends, spouses, brothers and sisters.

Isaiah 49:24-25 (KJV) says, "Shall the prey be taken from the mighty, or the lawful captive delivered? But thus saith the Lord, Even the captives of the mighty shall be taken away, and the prey of the terrible shall be delivered: for I will contend with him that contendeth with thee, and I will save thy children."

The same verses in the New International Version say, "Can plunder be taken from warriors, or captives rescued from the fierce? But this is what the Lord says: Yes, captives will be taken from warriors, and plunder retrieved from the fierce; I will contend with those who contend with you and your children I will save."

I have prayed in desperation for a way to penetrate the spirit world and tear Satan's hold from captives. I wanted to know how to reach into the fire. It was not until I began to pray in the understanding of binding and loosing that I felt empowered to tear backsliders out of Satan's grasp. After binding and loosing, I have seen rigid people become flexible—people who were hard to the gospel, refusing one word of spiritual help. There was no possible way of approaching them on the level of flesh and blood. The battle for these intractable souls had to be fought "behind their backs" in the spiritual world.

It is important to remember that we war not against flesh and blood. My youngest daughter loved the Lord with her whole heart as a child. As she entered her teen years, rebellion began to surface in her. Her reactions to mistakes I had made in raising her began to flare out of control. I forced her to attend church until she was seventeen, convinced she would eventually receive the truth if she was made to sit under it long enough.

I had the upper hand in the flesh, but I was not backing it up with spiritual warfare against the strongholds in her old nature. The enemy was accessing these strongholds and feeding her anger and hurt to drive her to rebellion against me and God. When she turned seventeen, I lost that battle in the flesh. Because I had not established territorial rights in the spirit world to hold onto her, she rebelled totally and bolted for the world.

Now I have learned to battle directly with the real troublemaker in the spirit world. This frees me from "needing" to point out where others are wrong and how they should know and do what God wants them to do. Most of those I pray for have all been in church and heard the Word, so I wasn't giving them unknown information. But there are clouds of blindness affecting their spiritual vision right now. I am far more dangerous to the enemy and effective for them by loosing the effects of that blindness and the strongholds in their lives. The prayers of binding and loosing are bringing them to the point where they can see the light for themselves once again.

The battle is on for many souls that I love, but none seem to be aware or resentful of it. They appear to think

I have mellowed and accepted them the way they are. Ha! I have no intention of accepting any status in their lives until all of them walk into the kingdom of God. I have made my declaration to the enemy and I have made my stand. There will be no summit meetings, no negotiations, no treaties with him where my loved ones are concerned!

I'm redeemed, I'm blood bought and I'm part of the Church of Jesus Christ and the gates of hell shall not prevail against me. In His name and by His power, I will not quit until every captive is brought back home!

There is a great praise song out right now that says we are not maintaining and we will not compromise, we are marching into the battle where only the strong survive. Well, stronger is He who is in me than he who is in the world! <u>I know</u> who's going to survive.

Far-Reaching Implications

There are far-reaching implications of the power of this way of praying. God tells us to pray for leaders and kings and even nations, such as the command to pray for the peace of Israel. The Apostle Paul said, "I urge, then, first of all, that requests, prayers, intercession and thanksgiving be made for everyone—for kings and all those in authority..." (1 Tim. 2:1-2 NIV).

Bind those who are in authority to the things of God and then loose the wrong attitudes and patterns of thinking that have so deceived world leaders and government officials. If ever there was a need to strip away strongholds and the blindness and error they protect, it is from those who are making incredibly far-reaching decisions in these perilous last days. Bind the President of the United States, the heads of other countries, the governor of your state, the supervisors of your county and the leaders of your city to the will of God and to the truth. Bind their feet to paths of righteousness. Jesus said that whatsoever we would bind on earth would be bound in heaven.

Loose wrong patterns of thinking, attitudes, beliefs, ideas, desires, habits and behaviors from them. Loose the power and effects of the words of wrong counsel given to them. Loose the ideas of man from them. Loose tradition and generational bondages from them. Loose the power and effects of word curses spoken to them, about them and by them. Whatsoever you loose on earth, by the power and authority of Jesus Christ, will be loosed in heaven.

Apply these principles in your prayers to impact Israel's tension-filled situation and circumstances today. Pray for the deliverance and salvation of the Jewish people. In Isaiah 27:3-4 (TAB) the Lord says, "I, the Lord, am its (Israel's) keeper. I water it every moment; lest anyone harm it, I guard and keep it night and day. Wrath is not in Me. Would that the briers and thorns (the wicked internal foe) were lined up against Me in battle! I would stride in against them, I would burn them up together."

Then He says in verse 5, "Or else (if all Israel would escape being burned up together there is but one alternative), let them take hold of My strength and make complete surrender to My protection, that they may make peace with Me! Yes, let them make peace with Me!"

The Lord always stands ready to do battle over and for Israel. Yet if unbelieving Israel is to escape the coming destruction that stands even now at her borders, the Jewish people must take hold of His strength, the truth, His will and make peace with their Messiah. <u>As you pray for Israel</u> in whatever way the Holy Spirit would lead you, bind the leaders, the inhabitants and the Jewish people all over the world to the will of God, the truth and the keeping, saving blood of Jesus Christ which was shed for them.

Bind their feet to paths of righteousness, bind their minds to the mind of Jesus Christ and bind them to the work of the cross in their lives. Loose the wrong patterns of thinking, attitudes, beliefs, traditions and generational bondages, deceptions, behaviors and wrong plans of men from them. Strip the clouds blinding their minds that they cannot see the light of the gospel of Jesus Christ, their Messiah. Tear down the strongholds that have imprisoned their minds for centuries. Pray for the deliverance of Israel and the Jewish people.

And finally—bind believers everywhere to a desire for revival. Loose hindrances and strongholds from them that are blocking the way and allowing no room for revival to occur.

SUMMARY

1. Whether or not an individual wants help is not the issue. Strongholds keep them from wanting help and strongholds can be dealt with through loosing!
2. Those who refuse help are "not in their right minds," which can be dealt with by binding their mind to the "right mind," the mind of Christ.
3. It is God's will that "whosoever" should be saved. Since Satan's goal is to control man's will, you can best thwart his efforts by binding "whosoever's" will to the will of God.
4. Those under the blindness of the enemy either do not recognize truth any longer or never knew it. Binding them to truth helps them to "see."
5. When you pull others out of the fire, binding stabilizes them and loosing strongholds keeps them from returning there.
6. Binding and loosing can shatter and destroy the effects of mistakes you made as a parent, including those now affecting grandchildren as well.
7. Binding and loosing prayers can impact world leaders, government officials and Israel. Use them to bind all Christians to desire for revival.

CHAPTER 10

Yes, It Really Works!

If I had to try to condense this book into one sentence, I would say its contents have come from learning how to apply the keys of binding and loosing to the human soul. Jesus said He would give the keys of the kingdom to us and we could apply them to <u>whatsoever</u> (Matt. 16:19, 18:18), a very big word. We have been unaware of the enormous scope of the power in binding and loosing long enough. It is time to set free all of the new creatures who have been imprisoned by self-imposed limitations.

There is a saying, "I have seen the enemy and it is me." Man is his own worst enemy, the devil is not. Satan has been defeated and must bow to the living and written Word. Yet we've spent an inordinate portion of our Christian lives hiding from, running from or fighting with Satan. We have allowed him to steal large amounts of precious, unredeemed time from us.

He has tricked us with mirrors, playing games with our minds and our sight. He has been like the Wizard of Oz, confusing and baffling us with smoke screens while he convinced us he had the power to control our destiny. And all the while, the real enemy has been our own soulish nature.

One of man's finest excuses regarding his failures has always been: "The devil made me do it!" Well, I have a prophetic bulletin about that which is straight out of the Word of God. God removes that "excuse" when He has the angel bind Satan with a great chain and throw him into the bottomless pit for 1,000 years after the battle of Armageddon. Think of it, mankind will live a devil-free existence on earth for 1,000 years!

Surely after the entire Book of Revelation has been fulfilled in every way right through the battle of Armageddon, man will realize that God was telling the truth all along. And when man has been given 1,000 years with no one trying to interfere with his relationship with Christ, man will learn to fully trust God's truth. Man will finally be able to "get it right," won't he?

Revelation 20:7 says Satan is released at the end of the 1,000 years and he goes right out and deceives the nations of the entire world all over again. He gathers an army whose numbers will be like the grains of sand on the seashore (Rev. 20:8) for yet another rebellion against God. Mankind has 1,000 devil-proof years to get a relationship right with God and millions still don't. Satan isn't our problem! But, trust me on this, he knows exactly what our problem is and he knows how to use it to bring destruction.

Satan is the destroyer who would like to kill us, steal from us and destroy us, but he is powerless over the believer unless he can get the believer's cooperation. We have a sure word from the Lord that when we resist the devil, he must flee. It is only when we fail to resist him or keep giving him open doors of access that he is able to attack us. Many have used the keys of binding to survive Satan's continuing efforts to destroy them. Yet, binding Satan and his demons is only a temporary, front-line defense for surviving. Survival and victory are not synonymous!

Binding and loosing function most effectively and permanently when applied to our own human soul and the old nature. The keys of the kingdom are the most powerful when they are used to strip away what causes us to oppose ourselves instead of opposing Satan. We cannot continue to oppose ourselves and be overcomers. A house divided against itself will always fall. We must be whole and fixed and steady in our stand.

This is difficult to accomplish in the natural realm in today's troubled times. Voices cry out all around us to distract us. Someone, somewhere at all times, is saying this group or that is being denied their rights. It doesn't matter to many whether their rights infringe upon someone else's rights or not. Individual rights not held up to the sword of the Word of God are almost always satisfied at the expense of someone else. Regardless of the insanity of some of the excesses, each of these groups is crying out for certain things that make "sense" to the old nature. This is why so many are caught up in them.

I must confess it would not be difficult to identify with some of these causes if I still had old patterns of thinking and was not using the Word of God to help me keep things in perspective. There are even some militant Christian groups operating out of old, soulish patterns of thinking today, though they believe they are marching perfectly in step with the will of God.

Jesus is the Head

Jesus is supposed to be the head over everything. Obviously, the majority of those living on the earth have rejected His headship, hence the state of the world today. First Corinthians 12:12 opens the passage that describes the body of Christ as one body with many parts. Jesus is the head and His body is made up of many members who are not to say to Him or to each other, "I don't need you!" (verse 21).

In our natural bodies, our head is very aware of what is going on with all of the members of the body. It immediately knows when a toe has been stubbed or a finger has been smashed or a muscle has been pulled. Jesus knows exactly the same thing about every member of His body. I believe He feels every injury and hurt and moves at once to give help, but the Word sent to bring healing is often blocked by the members themselves.

Our own natural members receive instructions and motor stability from the head which houses our brain. When something renders a certain member incapable of receiving, that member becomes incapacitated or spastic. The same thing has happened today to those who have rejected instructions and direction from the headship of

Christ. Many have become spiritually, emotionally and mentally incapacitated or spastic—ranging from one extreme of total apathy to the other extreme of violence.

As a headless world's political, economic and social order continues on, carnality, pride, lust, fear, frustration, failing economies and greed abound. The resulting incapacitation and spastic behaviors have brought about many wrong attitudes. One of the most dangerous attitudes is that someone else must pay for every offense, loss or hurt suffered. This has brought about physical and character assassinations, murders, robberies, lawsuits and retaliations of all magnitudes for perceived as well as real losses and offenses.

God's People Have the Answers!

The world is crashing around us and God's people are supposed to have the answers. Well, God's people do have the answers! There needs to be some renovation, some tearing down and some new putting on, but God's people are going to be used in these final days. We're not supposed to be hiding in our homes, washing our robes and pressing out the wrinkles in them, listening for His voice. We're supposed to have already taken care of our spiritual dry cleaning.

We're to be out there in the streets and in the byways when we're not on our knees. No matter where we end up going or what we end up doing, if we're giving help and answers and direction and hope to others, we'll hear His voice when it's time to go!

The world needs us right now. If someone hadn't taken the time to believe and pray and talk with you, where would you be? As Christians, we need to be ready and willing to give what we have been given. I used to have a lot of difficulty with people who seemed to be always needing attention and emotional support. I think the world has the same impatience most of the time. After I had been stripping old attitudes and patterns of thinking from myself for several months, I was quite surprised at my reaction to these same people.

Attitudes of Compassion

A young woman I'll call Bonnie poured out a bizarre and shocking story to me of the ugliest kind of abuse and neglect. I was quite concerned and prayed daily for her as well as trying to provide emotional support. A friend of mine said one day, "Did it ever occur to you that Bonnie might have made up that whole story just to get your sympathy and attention?" At one point in my life, I would have stopped and realized this was a distinct possibility as there was no way I could validate Bonnie's story. I probably would have suspected my friend was right and Bonnie was using me and pulled away. That was my old pattern of thinking.

To my surprise, I heard myself reply, "What if she did? It is really tragic if she felt she had to go to such an extreme to generate any concern for herself. If she did make the story up, she must be incredibly confused and hurting inside. So it doesn't really matter—either way, she needs understanding." I was genuinely amazed at this new attitude I had acquired from Jesus.

I now cringe inwardly, sometimes outwardly confronting, when I hear someone say, "He's only looking for attention" or "she's just having a pity party" or "he's feeling sorry for himself again." At one time or another, we've all said or thought these things to justify distancing ourselves from another person's needs. Extreme attempts to get attention show unmet needs of a great magnitude. Which one of us would write off someone's visible needs if they were crying for attention as they lay broken and bloodied beside a freeway?

As you pray in this new understanding, look expectantly above and beyond your old patterns of reacting to people. Do not be afraid to offer yourself and the God inside of you. God wants to use your arms to hug them. God wants to use your voice to speak words of wisdom and hope to them. God wants to use your heart to love them. We all need to create room in ourselves for that kind of boldness and wisdom and love. Jesus always stretched himself to reach out to those in need.

To be understanding, we need to see others as God sees them. If He values their potential, how can we judge them as worth as any less? Realize there are times when your understanding may be the only tangible link an abusive spouse, a rebellious teenager, an angry young man or an impossible neighbor may have to God. Be willing to get outside of your own skin.

Sound dangerous? Let me to return to the "parable" or word picture of the baby bound by the body wrap to the parent. The little one is bound to the back or the chest (near the heart) of the parent for its own safety and well-being. Ultimately, the baby grows and matures and, as a child, is allowed more freedom. At times the child is bound only by the voice and close attention of the parent. The bond is still there, but it is less tangible. It becomes more an element of love, trust and the child's ability to have listened and learned.

If the child fails to heed the voice of the parent, the parent wisely restricts the child and again goes over the importance of listening. The child ventures out once more, knowing he or she can always return to the arms of the parent to be reassured of the security, safety and love there. It is up to the parent to determine the type of the bond, knowing when the child must be tucked close or can be allowed to walk into new experiences tethered by words of love and guidance.

I am safe and secure when I am in my Father's will. I can be held in His arms in private times and I can walk out into my world tethered by His voice and love when there are plans and purposes to fulfill. I want Him to choose whether my position will be one of resting, warring or reaching out. With my will bound to His, I can just flow with the forward motion of our relationship.

To experience Jesus Christ's reaction to situations I walk into, I have bound myself to His mind so I will not react from a purely human perspective. To freely receive the Holy Spirit's guidance, I have bound myself to His truth and the blood of Jesus and everything good and stable and strong.

I bind my loved ones to God's will and truth and the mind of Christ. I loose the strongholds from them, disrupting and destroying the deceptions and lies the enemy has offered them for so long. I want everything I can get from God for myself and for my loved ones and

I believe He wants to give it. I'm under construction, being renovated, a restoration project! I'm hauling out the old and receiving the new. I'm building foundations for my loved ones' renovation at the same time.

Smaller Area Renewals

There has been some major remodeling in my life since I began praying this way, but some very precious, smaller "area" renovations have also been exciting. I was bothered for several years with arthritis that continued to get worse. I had been repeatedly warned that my excessive intake of coffee (often up to fifteen cups on a particularly stressful day) was bad for arthritis. I knew this was probably true, but I liked coffee and did not consider caffeine a sin. There are many things that are not sin which are still not good for us.

I had run across several old folk-medicine references that drinking raw apple cider vinegar and unprocessed natural honey was beneficial in dissolving painful acid crystals involved in arthritis in the joints. Although it seemed to have a ring of truth to it, I never tried it. I struggled through my days with a lot of pain, taking enormous amounts of aspirin, which made my stomach hurt all the time, which made me eat too many antacids, and so on.

After binding and loosing for a few months, I noticed the middle finger of my right hand was beginning to twist. No longer was the arthritis just something to stoically bear, it was beginning to deform my hands which are directly connected to my livelihood as a writer. God had been trying to show me the truth of bad eating habits for some time. Suddenly it was TRUTH in bright neon letters!

I instantly cut my coffee intake to one or two cups a day, something I had never been able to do before without headaches and irritability. I experienced none of the usual withdrawal symptoms. I began to drink raw honey and raw apple cider vinegar in hot water every morning. I reduced my sugar intake until I found I could almost do without any refined sugar at all. In less than a week, most of my symptoms of arthritis began to disappear. I cut my aspirin intake to nearly zero and my stomach was so grateful. Because I was no longer in constant pain, I purchased a wonderful exercise machine to use. I feel great and my fingers are flexible and well.

As I began to cut my sugar intake, I recognized that I had been using sugar to deal with stress. I stashed extra sweets in pockets, purse and desk drawers whenever I anticipated stress—sort of like a squirrel hiding nuts for the winter. I was using sugar as a coping mechanism.

Bound to truth, I finally began to deal spiritually with my stress through binding and loosing prayers. I reduced my sugar to almost zero with no withdrawal symptoms. I have experienced several healings in my body since that time. We often block our own healings because of destructive habits we refuse to acknowledge and quit. If you insist upon repeatedly thrusting your hand into the fire when God has told you not to, He isn't going to heal your burns!

Binding and Loosing and Healings

I know the surface of the potential of binding and loosing prayers for physical healing has barely been scratched at this point. A close friend was recently diagnosed (following a mammogram) as having a strange-looking growth in her breast and a lumpectomy was ordered. In addition to the regular "training wheels" prayers she had been praying for nearly five months, I asked her to lay her hand on the afflicted area and begin binding that part of her body to the blood of Jesus and the will and purposes of God. We faithfully agreed in prayer several times before she went in for surgery.

Her biopsy results proved so unusual, the doctors proclaimed her to be an enigma. Six doctors were unable to agree on the biopsy findings and forwarded her tests to Stanford University for further research. Finally, two weeks after the surgery, the results came back. The "experts" said the tissue samples were unusual, indeed, but non-malignant. God knew that all along, but I think He got a little extra mileage out of those tests with the many who were involved.

During this same time period, another woman informed me she had already been diagnosed as having a cancerous growth in her breast. This woman has been praying the prayers of binding and loosing since early 1990. When we spoke, I told her to lay her hand over the afflicted area and bind that part of her body to the blood of Jesus and to the will and purposes of God each day until her scheduled lumpectomy. Concerned family members were amazed at the faith apparent in this woman's life as she neared the day of surgery, perhaps even a mastectomy.

When I checked with her just prior to her entering the operating room, she was quite calm as she told me, "I'm not worried. I know God is in control and whatever happens, He will take care of it." And, of course, He did! Seventeen lymph nodes were removed for testing and there was no sign of the malignancy in any of them.

Because of the type of cancer involved, the doctor felt it necessary to schedule daily radiation treatments for four weeks. After hearing several negative stories about radiation therapy, we again bound her and the treatments to God's will and purposes. Happily, she experienced no adverse reactions of any kind other than a minor fatigue following the final treatments.

Ungodly Thoughts

As I bind my mind to the mind of Christ, I am acutely aware of critical and judgmental thoughts about others. I still get them sometimes, but I recognize them, loose them and see them go. I used to feed on these thoughts in an attempt to meet my own sense of inadequacy and neediness. I no longer feel compelled to do this as so many of my needs have been met by the Lord himself.

Many Christians have trouble dealing with their thought life. Any suggestion by the enemy can be so subtle that believers can miss a wrong pattern of thinking sneaking in and establishing itself. They are oblivious until it has plunged them into anger, bitterness, despair or depression. Some thought patterns can become like raging forest fires if that first little flame remains unchecked. Binding yourself to the mind of Christ gives you a spiritual smoke detector that immediately picks up on any incendiary thoughts not from Him.

The alarm goes off and it is up to the believer to choose to loose the wrong thought. The only thing the believer must do is remain ready to choose to loose it. Some wrong thoughts can become so entrenched in the minds of certain people, they become habit forming. The person becomes addicted to the attitude, the memory or the pain and continually reruns the old internal videos to reinforce it. Loosing will break the strongest cycle of this type.

Binding and loosing brings freedom by creating room to receive God's truth and grace to cleanse and heal our wounds. The Word gives us no justification for thoughts based on the unfairness of life or any position from which to judge or punish others. That is God's position alone. We are responsible only for how we react to what has happened. God alone knows what He's doing in others' lives and we need to stay out of the area of judgment.

Not a Pain-Free Process

It's getting easier and easier to shed little pieces of embedded dirt and grit that I've been overlooking or justifying. And it is hurting less and less. This binding and loosing is not a pain-free process. But, living your life according to your own rules is certainly not a pain-free process, either. When you bind yourself to the things of God and pain comes, there are no parachutes that allow you to bail out, crying, "Changed my mind, God!" But pain associated with God's workings is always part of a healing process that will bring wholeness.

When you bind yourself to the steady and fixed things of God, you will find you can finally accept yourself as God does. God's acceptance and affirmation will be enough to make you feel validated even if the whole world seems to be wishing you'd just go away. Human approval might still be nice once in a while, but you'll know that your real validation comes from the One in heaven who will never withhold it if you fail to measure up.

Loosing wrong behaviors and habits will free you to walk in new spiritual motivation. Loosing old patterns of thinking will break unhealthy coping techniques. Loosing the strongholds you've erected will enable you to close open doorways from your past and seal them with the blood of Jesus. This can bring about last-ditch attacks of the enemy that will require you to stand firm on what you believe. You need to really want spiritual freedom, power and a deeper relationship with the Lord so you will be prepared to follow through.

Just Do It!

So, how complicated is all this? Do you need to know all the Greek and Hebrew previously quoted? No. I have had believers completely overwhelmed by the whole principle and unsure they could do it right, but wanting to "do it" anyway. Sarah's mother was one of the first, so I gave her a written prayer to read until she was comfortable. This was the beginning of the "training wheels" prayers. She began by reading the prayer and then Matthew 16:19 aloud. Within a period of time, she felt secure enough to pray from her heart without the written format.

Sarah felt very inadequate at first, so I gave her this extremely basic prayer on a piece of paper to read aloud:

"In the name of Jesus I bind myself to the will of God, the truth and the mind of Christ. I loose wrong patterns of thinking and attitudes, behaviors and habits, and strongholds from myself. Amen."

Sarah carried the piece of paper in her pocket until she felt secure enough to discard her "training wheels" and pray from her heart. Whereas Sarah had seemed to only regress during fifteen years of medical attention, spiritual advice and prayer, she began to experience deliverance within weeks of united prayer using these keys. Why?

Sarah had been in such bondage to wrong desires, beliefs, behaviors and their strongholds, she could not receive any answers. She was hardly able to receive anything from God at all because of the multiple strongholds she had erected—strongholds she believed to be her only security.

Every Scripture read and every prayer prayed had all been building toward Sarah's deliverance, but the keys of binding and loosing freed her to begin to receive it. God's Word will never return unto Him void, it will always accomplish the purpose for which He sent it. This is truth. Sarah finally allowed the Word to begin to accomplish its purpose in her life.

Changing Lives

You can change your life and you can change the lives of others through these keys to the kingdom. You can bind a devastated, hurting individual to the things of God and know it is just as if you had rescued a hurting child from snarling, wild dogs and set it safely out of their snapping jaws. You can know wrong understandings and beliefs are being exposed and their protective strongholds undermined as you loose and shatter wrong things in others' lives.

You can be very effective in changing lives. You can set captives free. You can redeem precious time that has been wasted in trying to defend against the enemy's attacks.

You'll feel so free, you will not know where to start living in victory first! You'll be more precious, valuable and dangerous than you've ever been—precious to God, valuable to your family, your friends, your church and your community, and *dangerous* to the enemy.

SUMMARY

1. This book has come from learning how to personally apply the keys of binding and loosing to the human soul to set our new creatures free.
2. Satan has been like the Wizard of Oz, using smoke screens to convince us he has the power to control our destiny. Our real enemy has always been our own soulish nature.
3. Many have used keys of binding as only a temporary, front-line defense. The permanent answer is to strip away what causes us to oppose ourselves.
4. Jesus is supposed to be the head over everything. The majority of humanity has rejected His headship, living incapacitated or spastic lives.
5. The world is crashing and Christians are supposed to have the answers. God's people might still be under renovation, but they do have the answers!
6. Binding and loosing creates room to receive God's cleansing and healing. It makes room for love and forgiveness regardless of what others have done.
7. You can become very effective in changing lives, setting captives free and redeeming precious time previously wasted in fighting the enemy.